IS oasis for you?

25 stories from people who said yes!

Introduction by
MILLIE GRENOUGH
Author of *OASIS in the Overwhelm*

Edited by
CECILE WIJNE KROON

is oasis for you?
25 stories from people who said YES!

Published by Beaver Hill Press
orders@beaverhillpress.com
www.beaverhillpress.com

Cover design by Nicole Fitzgerald
Original OASIS logo by Elements LLC
Interior design by Dorothy Scott
Illustrations by George Herrick

The information contained in this book is intended for informational purposes only. If you have questions regarding a medical condition, please consult your health professional.

Library of Congress Cataloging-in-Publication Data
Grenough, Millie & Wijne Kroon, Cecile
is OASIS for you? 25 stories from people who said YES!

ISBN 0-9778411-5-4

1. Body/Mind. 2. Corporate. 3. Life Coaching. 4. Military. 5. Neuroplasticity. 6. Stress Management.
I. Grenough, Millie. II. Wijne Kroon, Cecile. III. Title. IV. Herrick, George—illustrations

what people are saying about OASIS

"There is practical and simple information available in this book to help restore you on your journey through life."

> **Bernie Siegel,** MD, Author, *Love, Medicine & Miracles*
> and *365 Prescriptions for the Soul*

"An excellent guide for Type A people like me who want quick and practical methods to manage stress. They really work!"

> **Brad Aldrich,** President, Aldrich + Elliott, PC,
> Consulting Engineers, Essex Jct., VT

"...lovely, clear and practical."

> **Esperanza Diaz,** MD, Medical Director, Hispanic Clinic;
> Associate Professor of Psychiatry, Yale University School of Medicine

"What I've read makes me feel like you know me, and you're writing about my life."

> **Nancy Weber,** Author, *What I See*

"I think I could use your book as a constant reference during my days."

> **Woody Powell,** Executive Director, Veterans for Peace

"For us recovering workaholics, Millie provides an invaluable service by coaching us to become more effective in the workplace while also helping us to fit work into a more appropriate place in the framework of our lives."

> **David Nee,** Former Executive Director,
> William Caspar Graustein Memorial Fund

"Looking for bits of balance in the daily chaos? Millie's OASIS Strategies give you short, sixty-second breaks from the zaniness of life—and, as a bonus, they're practical ideas to be happier."

Jim Donovan, Author, *Handbook to a Happier Life: A Simple Guide to Creating the Life You've Always Wanted*

"Millie Grenough's work is on the leading edge of dynamic health for those attempting a breakthrough into their own inner expression. Her work has helped people internationally for years, and I have experienced her dynamism as both a client and a colleague."

David Darling, Cellist, Composer; Founder, Music for People

"This is not only a beautiful book about how to find peace in a hectic life; it is also an inspiring story about life lessons. The author's resilience in the face of tragedy inspired a beautiful and easy manual to help the reader reclaim peace and health. Millie writes an easy to read, fast to apply book that can fit even the busiest reader."

Luis Añez, PsyD, Yale University School of Medicine

"This reads as smooth as a Japanese river stone. So easy to read, I wanted to read through to the end."

Bonnie Muller, LCSW, Certified Rubenfeld Synergist

"Millie has done an outstanding job illuminating the reality of the pressures of today and has provided a great recipe and guide in aiding us all on how to develop that personal oasis we all know we need. Thank you for helping me find my oasis. I needed that!"

Barry Foster, Founder, The Corporate Coaching Center

"Millie Grenough's four gentle, scientific, and simple exercises will give strength and shape to the future you, who will look back and thank today's you for wising up and finding simple paths to healthy body and soul."

Sidney MacDonald Baker, MD, Author, *Detoxification & Healing* and *The Circadian Prescription*

"I use the 3-B-C strategy regularly now and have noticed a definite and immediate improvement as I move through my hectic days managing my staff."

Ginger Mierzejewski, Manager, American Payment Systems

"Recognizing and 'voicing' our stresses, like our prejudices, enables us to deal with them and take action. *OASIS in the Overwhelm* acknowledges that while stress is a part of life there is a need to rest and recharge one's batteries, if only for a few minutes."

Elise Klein, Founder, Teachers Against Prejudice

"Millie Grenough offers a welcome oasis to our crazy pace. Grenough brings her vast academic and personal experience full circle to offer four simple skills that can be applied anywhere by anybody."

Jane Larson de Torras, Language Consultant, Barcelona

"Let me just say that I LOVE the title of the book. As soon as I read that I felt more at peace. The word alone is something of a mantra, immediately conjuring up feelings of peace and sanctuary. I LOVE it."

Mimi Houston, Freelance Writer, Mother of three young children

"I plan on buying your book for others because it presents simple and sensible strategies to create serene space in our lives. That's worth sharing."

Cyn Chegwidden, MBA, Field Marketing Manager for Military MBA

"One of the reasons I think many people will love OASIS is that it simply organizes various thoughts, methods and practices that people like me have been using in a desultory fashion to try to keep sane."

Anne Tyler Calabresi, Community Volunteer

"Any new book about stress and how to cope with it in our increasingly complex world must be welcomed with open arms. OASIS suggests simple steps that anyone of any age or walk of life can master. It works."

Elayne Phillips, Theatre Director, Swiss Musical Theatre Academy

"With four simple strategies to refresh your perceptions in an oasis of calm, Millie Grenough is offering nothing less than the opportunity and means to change your life—for the better."

David L. Katz, MD., FACPM, FACP
Author, *Disease Proof*; Medical Contributor, ABC News;
Columnist, *The New York Times* Syndicate

"In our high-speed, busy culture, we are all yearning for balance and ways to better manage our stress. Millie has brought the OASIS to us. Her strategies are valuable, practical, only take a minute. Every home and organization should have a copy!"

Carole Jacoby, Master Certified Coach; President, Life Visions

...about the *28 Day Guide*

"If you're serious about calming down and creating your own personal oasis, you don't want to miss the *28 Day Guide*. Filled with simple ideas and lots of inspiration, it's the perfect companion to *OASIS in the Overwhelm* and is sure to keep you on track."

Wendy Battles, The Clean Eating Coach, Healthy Endeavors

"The *OASIS 28 Day Guide* serves as the healing touch and genuine reminder of the truth that centers me daily in my hectic and often overwhelming life. It is a practical guide with real life-giving answers to cope and respond to our ever-changing existence."

Jane Petrozzi, Single mom of school-age child, Full-time Project Manager

"The *OASIS 28 Day Guide* is simple, in the sense of being a really doable process to commit to, and rich at the same time. I love the powerful questions you ask and the inspirational quotes and affirmations. I especially like the piece in the *tune in often* section where you suggest choosing a strategy for different stress scenarios. I'm going to copy and post that as a reminder for myself."

Jackie Rubell Johnson, CPCC, Choice Business and Personal Coaching, LLC

"The OASIS Strategies are easy, effective, and bring results. The *28 Day Guide* keeps you on track to achieve more calm and less chaos in just one month!"

Monica Tari, Therapist, Life Coach

...about the DVD: *Got Chaos? Get Calm!*

"WOW! Overwhelmed by the Oasis! Our world needs the message in this DVD. Watching it, my breathing deepened and heart rate slowed. A true oasis."

Margaret Longhill, President Emerita,
Will McLean Foundation for Florida Heritage in Music

"Invigorating—plus some! Millie G.'s voice is engaging. The well-chosen music sets the tone for each and every activity… The activities are just the right length. There is something for everyone, including youth. After all, we all have some chaos in our lives. And we all long for calm."

Freda Byron, Educator, Bermuda & Connecticut

"Only the best! This video brings Millie's work directly to you. If you can't see Millie in person or attend one of her seminars, this is the best alternative. I have used her techniques for many years and this is a proven method to 'Get Calm.'"

Thomas G. Campbell, Senior Vice-President, Sales, King Printing, Lowell, MA

...about the OASIS Training

"The OASIS program is just what the doctor ordered—for me and for my clients! The excellent training and support provided by Millie Grenough on my OASIS journey has made an incredible impact in my life."

Steve Porcaro, Sales Coach, Authorized OASIS Facilitator

"Breathing a mere 60 seconds—gets me through the moment. Chaos and crisis have moved in like the spring and summer rains for nonprofits... But we have our breath, a gift from God. We have 60 seconds to center ourselves and use that gift. I can't tell you how appreciative I am for the illumination you put on taking just 60 seconds. Sometimes I can just get out only a 'North!' But it still helps."

Robert Page, LCSW, BCD, Authorized OASIS Facilitator

"I am thrilled, Millie, to be one of your first TeleClass Training participants. Your leadership and passion for your work radiated over the phone lines and I am inspired to keep using and spreading the strategies... Thank you, Millie."

Fiona Miller, PCC, Certified Retirement Options Coach,
Christchurch, New Zealand

"In today's complicated world, it is hard to find anything that is simple **and** impactful, that has benefits in both your personal and professional lives. OASIS provides my clients and me with strategies to move from overwhelm to empowerment, to living our best lives. It is amazing what you can accomplish once stress is managed. OASIS Strategies become a way of life... a good life."

Karen Senteio, Personal and Business Coach; President, VERVE, LLC

INTERNATIONAL AUTHOR, COACH AND MOTIVATIONAL SPEAKER
MILLIE GRENOUGH is best known for her *OASIS in the Overwhelm* books, training programs and workshops. Her 60-second Strategies for stress management have reached and helped thousands, all over the world. The OASIS Training Program has graduates in ten United States, and in Panama, Puerto Rico, and New Zealand.

An ex-nun turned nightclub singer, ex-shy Kentuckian turned international speaker, Millie inspires people to do what they thought was impossible, and reach their full potential—while becoming saner, healthier and happier. She knows that doing this, one tiny bit at a time, helps our world become a happier place.

Millie is a Clinical Instructor in Psychiatry at Yale University School of Medicine, a licensed Clinical Social Worker, certified in EMDR-Level II with a specialty in Performance Enhancement, and 2010 Coach of the Year in the Connecticut Chapter of the International Coach Federation.

e-mail: millie@milliegrenough.com
website: www.milliegrenough.com

contents

foreword

caught in the overwhelm?

I WAS. AND I AM SO HARD-HEADED that it took a near-death bicycle accident to make me stop my frantic lifestyle. That's when *my* OASIS journey began.

During my months of recuperation, I realized I had to find ways to heal myself before I re-entered the "real" world. In the quiet safety of my backyard hammock, I was able to ask myself those big questions that we often don't have time to ask: *Who am I?* and *What am I here on this planet for?*

I came up with four simple strategies that I could use anywhere and didn't cost a penny. Each of them took only 60 seconds. I called them my "oasis in the overwhelm." They worked! My colleagues noticed the change and wanted in on my secret. I began teaching the strategies to anyone looking for clarity and calm in this crazy existence of ours.

That first outreach has grown into the *OASIS in the Overwhelm* stress-management program, which has to date reached thousands of people on five continents. And hundreds have trained with me to become OASIS Facilitators.

In this book you will find stories of 25 of these people. They are from diverse cultures, different professional backgrounds, of varied ages, all walks of life—from life coaches to US Army personnel, harried parents to critical care nurses. Each of them journeyed to reach their own OASIS, and it has changed their lives.

You will read how they use the OASIS Strategies to ride life's small waves and large tsunamis to enjoy greater health and happiness in their own lives. More than that, they are bringing this resilient balance and peace to many, many others in all parts of the world.

Our day-to-day life in this 21st century is, in many ways, a perilous journey. Stress is everywhere, and with everyone. Medical experts say that we live now in a chronic state of high alert accompanied by an increased sense of helplessness. Not a great combo! Studies say that stress contributes to 80% of major illnesses, is responsible for 75-90% of visits to doctors' offices, and costs businesses as much as $300 billion a year.

That's the bad news. The good news? We do not need to be helpless victims regarding stress. The latest neuroscience verifies that how we respond to stress makes all the difference. That's where OASIS comes in.

The essence of OASIS is not to eliminate stress. If we did that, we would be dead. Rather, it is to help us interact consciously—and with clarity—with what is on our plate. In brief, to give us tools to be the CEO of our own lives. I love the words of Hans Selye, the grandfather of stress physiology: *Stress is the spice of life.* If you are a cook, you know what that means. Too much spice = disaster. Too little spice = blah.

The 25 authors in this book are definitely not blah people. And their lives are anything but boring. I hope that their stories inspire you so that you, too, find deeper peace and more vibrant enjoyment in the minutes of your day-to-day life.

An extra note for you/us high-energy folks: *Calm does not mean comatose.* As Hans Selye reminds us: Stress *is* the spice of life. How we use it is the decisive factor.

how to get the most out of this book

🌴 **Jump in wherever you wish.** Flip through the pages and see what attracts your eyes. Maybe a person's photo will grab you, or a title, or just a word. Trust your fingers, your eyes, your gut.

🌴 **Learn more about the four key OASIS Strategies** that the authors refer to. Go to pages 236-243 for illustrated guidance.

🌴 **Pause every once in a while just to exhale.** Ease into the stories and give yourself the opportunity to experience your own refreshment, repose, rejuvenation.

🌴 **Try a strategy yourself.** Just do it! As the Chinese proverb says:

> Tell me and I'll forget.
> Show me and I may remember.
> Involve me and I'll understand.

Millie

introduction

got a minute?

THAT'S ALL IT TAKES to change your life. 60 seconds. Really.

I realize that those words may sound like airy-fairy baloney. But when you think about it, this minute is all we really have. And it is followed by *this minute*... and *this minute*... and *this minute*. How we use *this minute* makes all the difference in the world to us, and to everyone around us. It's as simple as that. And that's what OASIS is about.

What *is* an oasis? My Syrian friend Simon reminds me that *oasis* is originally from the Coptic language. It refers to a specific fertile place in the Libyan Desert that offers refreshing water to those who are thirsty, safety for those in danger, and a place of comfort, companionship and rest for anyone exhausted from the journey.

The aim of this book is exactly the same: to offer you refreshment, safety, comfort, and companionship on your journey. I am thrilled to bring these 25 stories to you. The authors let you know what brought them to OASIS, and how they right now are sharing it with others. I am humbled and incredibly grateful when I realize how the simple power of OASIS is rippling out to places I have never been, to people I have never met. This is how change works. One person at a time, one minute at a time, one simple act at a time.

from crash to clarity

MY BICYCLE ACCIDENT was what my mom would have called "a blessing in disguise." Little did I know then what far-reaching consequences that unexpected flip over the handlebars would have. As I lay unconscious on that Connecticut country road, my shocked brain must have already been initiating its own improved re-wiring.

At that time I knew nothing about the science of neuroplasticity, about how our brains can re-wire themselves towards greater health. It was only later that I stumbled upon the amazing research of Richard Davidson, Jeffrey Schwartz, and tons of other scientists. I was elated. Their research verifies what I witness happening when people use the OASIS Strategies: they are literally re-wiring their brains away from anxiety, agitation, depression, and towards calm, clarity and compassion.

I am astounded by the response to OASIS. Today, thousands of people on five continents, ages 3 to 93, use OASIS to find resilient balance. Why are so many people drawn to the strategies? I believe it is for four simple reasons: they are quick and easy, don't cost a penny, are highly adaptable, and—most important—they work.

In this book, you will get a glimpse of the many different ways people use OASIS in their own lives and how they share it with others.

Where to begin? Take your pick.

on the front lines

ANGELA McGRADY AND HOWARD REYES WORK WITH US ARMY personnel. They were in a two-day training *Trauma and Mindfulness* that I conducted at Fort Sam Houston in San Antonio, Texas for US Army personnel working in Afghanistan, Iraq, Korea, and at bases throughout the USA. ANGELA, an Air Force veteran and Compassion Fatigue Educator, brings her gifts to veterans, their families, and the hard-working staff who are under constant pressure to meet the dire needs of their clients. Angela reveals that the Cue-2-Do strategy is her personal favorite, whether she's working with a vet with PTSD or at home with her teenagers.

HOWARD also works in a high-stress job. With an OASIS colleague, Howard developed a program at the Warrior Transition Battalion in Schofield Barracks, Hawaii. Their program, to help staff defuse their own stress so they could be more available to themselves and to the people they serve, won a national *Psychologically Healthy Workplace Award*. Howard also uses an occasional 4-D strategy when he is in heavy traffic or other jams.

SHEILA KEARNEY has a different front line: teens in inner-city Bridgeport, CT. After a long career as an executive manager in the private sector, Sheila says, "I made a vow to seek opportunities to teach and inspire young, diverse and at-risk students." OASIS is helping her do that. Sheila creates variations of the strategies to invite overwhelmed adolescents, some of them single mothers, to gain control of their spiraling lives and experience moments of peace for themselves.

on the beauty front

TANISHA AKINLOYE HAD A CAREER as owner of a successful beauty business. She says that her clients helped her realize they needed more than just outward beauty. Tanisha dug deep into her wisdom to create *Empowering Through Beauty*, an organization that offers homeless women and women in prison a fresh start for the next chapters in their lives. The "fresh start" includes enhanced self-esteem and better ways to deal with stress, as well as cosmetic makeovers.

ANN REEVES is a wizard at connecting people with the beauty of nature to restore and refresh themselves. She leads women on outdoor retreats and weaves art, nature and OASIS together to minimize stress and enhance vitality. A psychologist and artist, Ann is adept at inventing custom-made strategies to meet the specific needs of ADHD and other children she works with. A simple tool often creates a shift from anxiety/low self-esteem to focus and pleasure in learning.

GEORGE HERRICK focuses his attention on another challenge: recovery from addiction. A recovering addict himself, George clearly recognizes the strong pull of old habits, and just as clearly recognizes the power we each have to develop new patterns. He delights in introducing people to the beauty of their own lives, whatever their current condition may be. Read how George used the 3-B-C to help his client "Frank" emerge from chaos and begin to see possibilities.

in critical situations

IN HER WORK IN THE NEO-NATAL INTENSIVE CARE UNIT at Montefiore Hospital in New York City, nurse SUSAN TOMS is constantly in the midst of high tension. When a newborn weighs only a few pounds, this is a shock for all concerned. Sue brings her experience and compassion to create a place of calm for distraught parents, teeny preemies—and for beleaguered staff. She knows that the right strategy, the right breath, at the right time, can be the difference between life and death.

VIRGINIA KRAVITZ'S passion is to guide clients to greater fulfillment and enjoyment in their lives. A member of the Pioneer OASIS group, she coaches people both in person and via phone. After a hurricane struck the island of Haiti, Ginny had the opportunity to help her client Vanessa move through this calamity. Meet Vanessa and read how she used a program that Ginny co-authored, the *28 Day Guide*, to regain her sense of joy in the aftermath of the overwhelming catastrophe.

SUZANNE ROSENBERG has years of experience in situations that call for clear thinking in critical times: hospice, palliative care, end-of-life decision making. She also knows the importance of using the strategies for herself, whether dealing with compassion fatigue or wrestling with the ordinary challenges of everyday life. Suzanne's story of how she used the Cue-2-Do in the parking lot to deal with an emergency of her own will tell you more about that.

Administrator of a home health/hospice agency in a large hospital, DEBRA HEALEY deals daily with crises. An accidental meeting with Millie led Debra to enroll in the OASIS Training for her own well-being. When she found that stress invaded the lives of her clerical staff as well as the bedside clinicians, she realized that her entire staff could benefit from the strategies. She brought OASIS to them and says that the *O to Go* packs provided her teams with portable reprieve.

how about stress and our bodies?

AWARENESS OF BODY + ATTENTION TO BREATH: **MARJORIE POLYCARPE** appreciates that in OASIS. A longtime nurse and yoga instructor, Marjorie knows that body and breath are crucial elements in the health of anyone, no matter their age or current physical condition. "The body knows, before the mind, when discomfort occurs," she notes. Marjorie integrates yoga with OASIS to enhance vitality; she is skillful at using the body to heal the whole person.

PETER HIMMEL'S experience as a medical doctor, combined with his curiosity about what makes us healthy or ill, gives him a unique perspective on the relationship between stress and disease. He investigates the *root causes*, not just the *symptoms*, of stress in individuals. Peter illuminates how trauma affects the physical and emotional health of children and adults, and how the OASIS Strategies may be used to alleviate the harmful consequences of trauma.

LYNNEA BRINKERHOFF gives hope to all of us: it's not how often we fall that matters; it's *how* we fall. An avid sportswoman, international coach, and student of Aikido, Lynnea knows the importance of when and how to breathe, when and how to release. She introduces us to *ukemi* so that we can fall with ease, and get up again, and again, and again. Lynnea's own breakthroughs, plus examples from basketball pros and police officers, give instruction to all us ordinary people.

care for others—and self

AS A HOLISTIC LIFE & WELLNESS COACH, **KAREN GOMEZ'S** dream is to take what she does "from the yoga room to the boardroom." Little did she expect that her 90-year-old mother, who has Alzheimer's, would introduce her to an entirely different audience. Karen relates how an inspired moment during an afternoon visit with her mom created an unforeseen opportunity for OASIS. In Karen's words, "I did not expect to bring it into assisted living facilities, and especially not to my mother."

VIRGINIA ANN GRIFFITHS faces the demands of being a wife, business woman, wife, and mother of four children, including teenage boys. She realizes that parents—both moms and dads—are, in her words, "over-extended, stressed, and feel that there's just not enough time for them." As a Parent Time Management Coach, Virginia Ann uses OASIS to help families deal with nitty-gritty daily trouble spots: how to prioritize, organize, and actually find enjoyment in being together.

The OASIS Training brought **DINA MARKIND**, an experienced nurse and certified coach, to a fresh realization of the supreme necessity of self-care, especially for those who care for others. In her study of the neuroscience that infuses OASIS, Dina gained even greater impetus to improve the physical and emotional health of care providers. She uses her skills to help them prevent—or come back from—burnout, and find greater joy in their lives.

RENEE O'CONNELL knows first-hand how difficult it is for parents to balance the multiple facets of their lives: managing her own work, her husband's consuming job, three pre-teen children who are involved in multiple activities. To respond to these issues, Renee organized the first *OASIS for Parents* meeting. She is OASIS' office manager and worldwide OASIS Community go-to liaison. Renee tells us how the strategies help her ride all these waves.

REBECCA SANTIAGO, President of the Hartford Chapter of the National Association of Hispanic Nurses, is second-generation Hispanic. She grew up in South Bronx turbulence—"gang wars, poverty, burning buildings, stray bullets..." Rebecca's ability to survive—as a young girl, a mother, now a grandmother—shapes how she embodies OASIS. When you read about her grandson Lucas and his green stone, you may wish that Rebecca was *your* grandmother.

in other places, with different cultures

WHEN MUBARAKAH IBRAHIM WAS ON THE OPRAH WINFREY SHOW, she remarked, "No matter where you choose to worship, all women want to know the same thing: how do you get rid of cellulite?!" She told Oprah that women everywhere have a common goal: to be healthy and to be their best selves. After teaching in Saudi Arabia, Mubarakah returned home to establish *Fit Haven*, to help *all* women—regardless of their income—learn to manage stress and become truly healthy.

SUZANNE DUDLEY-SCHON looks Scandinavian from her father's genes, but she describes herself as "Hispanic on the inside." She notes that on travels to her mother's native Dominican Republic, everyone she meets—"no matter the age, status, income, or job (waiter, guard, parent, or bank executive), they all have stress." Suzanne brings OASIS to a variety of audiences: health care professionals, domestic violence shelter volunteers, and—as needed—her own family.

OASIS in an actual desert? Pioneer Trainer ELANA PONET experienced just that. The summer following her training, she guided a group of college students on a tour of Israel. As they stopped to rest in the sandy Negev, Elana on impulse asked them each to pick up an object, look at it, and breathe. She remembers: "Sweet irony… in a place where stones are often thrown in anger and frustration, how lovely to imagine everyone doing the OASIS 1 Stone…"

Master Coach SUSAN SEIDMAN trains life and business coaches globally. At age 25 Sue left New York City to live in Puerto Rico and quickly became a pioneer of healthy innovation in her adopted land. She planted the seeds of coaching and Reiki on the Island. Along with Panamanian OASIS grad Dr. Caroline Cooke, Sue was instrumental in having OASIS translated into Spanish, and she is now training OASIS Facilitators. Sue's grand intention? "Bring the power of OASIS to as many Latin countries as I can."

and driven executives?

JILL BERQUIST WORKED FOR YEARS IN THE CORPORATE WORLD before beginning her own business. Her aim is to help high performers achieve their goals, but not sacrifice their health or souls in the process. Jill, co-author of the *28 Day Guide*, shares how she used OASIS breathing to help her executive client "Tom" release his vise-grip tension. She says that sometimes on a brutal day, he sends her a text: "Good day for breathing, coach."

KATHLEEN THOMPSON, an expert in finance, technology and process design, has weathered numerous mergers and reorganizations. A personal health crisis and family loss led her to OASIS. After Kathleen experienced benefits for herself, she formulated stress management tips to meet the specific needs of colleagues; her webinars have reached thousands in the high-pressure financial world. As a musician, Kathleen knows the importance of having our lives sing.

Corporate Training and Development Specialist KARIN JOY WHITLEY had to find practical ways to relieve stress in her energy industry. Recent happenings in the economy and her company placed increased strains on the physical and emotional wellness of many employees. Read Karin's chapter to see how she bypassed the usual obstacles—"I don't have time," and—especially for men—"I don't do that kind of thing"—by initiating speedy one-on-one meetings.

my journey—and yours

MY STORY, AS I TELL IT in my book *OASIS in the Overwhelm*, is what inspired many of the people you meet in these chapters. In that book, I promise:

- you can learn all four OASIS Strategies in one hour or less,
- you can use them immediately in your daily life at work and at home,
- they will make a positive difference in your life, and
- people around you will be glad you are using them.

The experiences of the many people who have used OASIS since then let me know that my promises remain true.

I warmly invite you to dive into OASIS to get a taste of what it might do for you. It is my deep hope that these stories lead you to greater health and more vibrant happiness. That's the best kind of balance in this busy world.

You have time.

You're right here, right now.

That's enough.

Go for it!

Millie

25 stories from people
WHO SAID *yes!*

KATHLEEN THOMPSON'S career is in the financial services industry, with roles from finance to technology and process design. She has participated in seven mergers and acquisitions, and several reorganizations. She experienced the death of her husband in 2004 and suffered a health crisis in 2011. Her quest to regain her health by redesigning her life from the ground up led her to become an OASIS Facilitator.

In addition to her job, Kathleen is a singer and directs music at her church. She has a blog and podcast, and teaches webinars to help professionals find their groove and make their lives sing.

e-mail: kthompson428@gmail.com
website: www.kathleenannthompson.com

the power of one

how i got started

I WAS ORIGINALLY DRAWN to the OASIS in the Overwhelm Strategies because they were quick and easy. Advertised as bringing calm in a chaotic world, these 60-second strategies were just what I needed to help calm my mind and help me to sleep. I bought the book and signed up for the OASIS Facilitator Training. This training is meant for those who wish to share these stress-management practices with others. I knew that everyone around me was stressed out, so figured if the tools worked for me, they were bound to work for everyone else I knew as well.

The training was only a few weeks away, so I quickly read the book and crammed as much information as I could into my brain. I arrived at the training class exhausted and with my head spinning. I met six other women who wanted to share this slice of peace with their communities. The first thing we did was to breathe and let ourselves just "be." We shared about ourselves, our lives, why we had come, what our dreams were. We learned how to incorporate the OASIS practices into our everyday lives, and share the techniques in our own unique way. We bonded together as a group, and encouraged each other in our journey.

one stone

THE TECHNIQUE I WAS MOST DRAWN TO was 1 Stone. Although I appreciate all four of the techniques, the 1 Stone has had the most impact on my life. The mechanics are simple:

1. Choose a stone that you like and hold it in the palm of your hand.

2. Experience the stone's weight, notice the colors, feel the texture, think about how long it has been on this earth, where it may have originally come from, and anything else about it.

3. Sit in a comfortable position that allows you to breathe deeply.

4. With your eyes open and focused on the stone, take ten deep, slow breaths. If your mind wanders, which is common, bring it back to the stone.

When finished, sit with the stone for a few moments and notice how you feel.

What I found was that this practice was a short form of meditation. By keeping my eyes opened and focused on the stone, I was able to stay focused. My mind was less likely to wander than it did when I tried to meditate. I also didn't fall asleep, which can easily happen when you have insomnia. The stone reminded me to be grateful for the gifts that I have. I was able to focus my thinking, and stop the racing thoughts.

I keep a stone on my desk at work that says "JOY." The stone reminds me to breathe deeply, that I have peace in the midst of the chaos, and that joy is a state of mind. Even looking at the stone invokes a sense of calm and brings a smile to my heart.

one minute

WHEN WE ATTEMPT TO MAKE CHANGE in our lives, we most often assume it must be huge in order to make a difference. We think we have to go from being a couch potato to winning an iron man competition in a few short months. Or meditate for two hours a day to have calm. Or starve ourselves to lose weight. What happens? We cannot cope with the amount of change. It takes too much energy. We are in pain. We crave the foods we used to eat. The effort to sustain it is too great for us, and we fail.

What if we abandon that all-or-nothing mentality? What if we choose to just shift our behavior a little bit? Study after study has shown that short, consistent practice has better results than the longer occasional effort. Consistency forms a habit, which often expands, resulting in even more profound change.

Each of the OASIS techniques can be done in sixty seconds—one minute. We can each carve one minute out of our schedule to do something healthy and fun. That one minute, repeated several times per day over a period of time, creates a new healthy habit, and can transform our lives—one minute at a time.

one moment

WE HAVE ONLY THIS MOMENT TO LIVE. The previous moment is gone, and the next one is yet to come. Each moment is a precious gift. Choosing to be fully present in each moment deepens our joy and connects us to others in a more meaningful way.

I have spent so much of my life living in the future—thinking and planning for what comes next. The practice of living in the present moment does not come naturally to me. As I use some of the 1,440 minutes of each day to practice focusing on the here and now, I am developing a habit that will lead to the reward of a more vibrant life in every respect. Food tastes better. My friendships are closer. Colors appear brighter. I hear music in bird song, a flowing brook, a child's laugh. I have redeveloped a child's sense of wonder. So simple, and yet not easy.

See, hear, touch, taste, and smell the here and now. Experience all that this moment has to offer. Most of the time, it is beautiful when we have eyes to see and ears to hear. Even when the situation is difficult or painful, being fully present allows us to make better decisions about how to move forward. Focus on whatever is true and right and lovely and noble and excellent. Live NOW.

one life

WE OFTEN THINK THAT ONE LIFE cannot make much of a difference. We denigrate our own uniqueness, and attempt to live like others. Or we live vicariously through our children, our friends, our favorite celebrity.

Each one of us has a unique blend of talents, personality, character, and style. We are one-of-a-kind. We matter. A lot. In his book *The Fred Factor*, Mark Sanborn writes about a postal carrier named Fred, who delivers mail in Mark's neighborhood. Fred is passionate about his ordinary job, turning it into something extraordinary. One man. Making a difference to his customers. Changing his world for the better. We don't have to be famous, wealthy, or powerful to make a difference. We just have to be "us." And care.

one community

WHEN I GRADUATED from the OASIS Training, I joined the OASIS Community. Before the training, I was not even aware that such a community existed. I thought that each of us would go back to our own lives, teach stress-management strategies to those around us, and have fond memories of our time in Millie Grenough's office practicing the OASIS techniques.

What I have experienced is rich relationships, encouragement, and support. We come from many walks of life: corporate executives, small business owners, life and business coaches, parents, caregivers, social workers, nurses, sales people, artists, and writers. As we share ideas and dreams and encourage each other, we are better equipped to help others with whom we share life. We in turn are creating communities of peace where we live. Each reaching out to those around us—offering the hand of fellowship, help in struggle, and an encouraging word.

the meaning of ONE

ONE STONE TO FOCUS. One minute to shift life's direction. One moment to savor. One life to fully live. One community to spread a vision for peace. The power of One.

MUBARAKAH IBRAHIM is the founder and Executive Director of *Fit Haven*, an AFAA Certified Personal Trainer, owner and head trainer of BALANCE fitness studio for women in New Haven, CT, Fitness Counselor and Authorized OASIS Facilitator, with a track record in business and innovative health and fitness programming for women.

Mubarakah's notoriety includes several TV appearances, among others on *The Oprah Winfrey Show* "Thirty-something in America." She is a contributing expert to *Prevention Magazine*, and appeared on the covers of *The New York Times, Chicago Tribune, The Hartford Courant* and *New Haven Advocate*. In July of 2012 and 2013 she was invited as a special guest of President Obama for her work with health and fitness for women, and given the honor of sitting next to him during her visit. Mubarakah lectures, promotes and conducts workshops on alternative health, fitness and healthy living.

e-mail: mibrahim@balancect.com
website: www.balancect.com

from oprah to a king to finding oasis: my path to creating a FIT haven

I WAS TALKING ABOUT STRESS with my friend Wendy Battles. Wendy and I are both very interested in helping people get healthier—she with nutrition and I with exercise. We were talking about how stress is such an important factor in both our fields. I told Wendy how many women came to me because they wanted to lose weight, and how they couldn't do it either because they were so stressed, or the fact that they were so stressed was one of the reasons they were gaining weight. Wendy suddenly stopped me and said, "You should really look into Millie's OASIS Training. It deals with stress in a positive way. And it gives you concrete things you can do to manage it."

the muslim "mother teresa"

AT THE TIME, WENDY DIDN'T KNOW how close to home her words were. I have experienced how stress affects people in a very personal and immediate way: through my mother. Mom always seemed to take other people's problems as her own. We didn't have a lot of money, but she would always invite people into our house to stay, to share lunch, whatever we had. She felt it was her mission to be there for everybody, to solve the problems of everyone. People called her "the Muslim Mother Teresa."

Although she did wonderful things, I as her child had an inside view on how much stress this put on her, and how the stress affected her diabetes. Because we didn't have good health care, she got no information about how to prevent or handle her condition. All she knew was that it was absolutely necessary for her to take her insulin shot in time, or she could collapse into insulin shock. My father had died when I was eleven, so she was raising the six of us by herself. If something happened to her, that would put all of us in danger. My mom taught me how to drive when I was 13. She said, "You need to learn how to drive, because if I pass out while I'm driving, you need to drive to the hospital."

I didn't know all the facts then, but what I know now, from my involvement in the health and fitness industries, is that stress is the major cause of what we see as disease. And I know for a fact that poor and minority communities are hit the hardest by health conditions like diabetes, obesity, high blood pressure, and heart disease. I have been a Personal Fitness Trainer for thirteen years, and I can tell you story after story about how people have turned their lives around by managing what I call the three key factors: physical exercise, nutrition, and stress management. No one told my mother about those things. She suffered from the effects of diabetes—glaucoma, neuropathy, an amputated foot—before she died.

I didn't realize this until she called me one day and asked, "Do you think I should go to this dietician the doctor said I should talk to?" I inquired, "Has no one ever referred you to a dietician?" She said, "No." I realized during that conversation that she had had diabetes for 25 years and she was never taught how to take care of herself. It had taken 25 years of suffering from diabetes before she received the beginning of an education on the importance of nutrition.

we can learn how to deal with it

ONE DAY I WAS LISTENING to a recording by Dr. Andrew Weil. He was talking about a young physician who was eager to solve the world's diseases. The young man went off to a remote village in Africa and thought he would cure malaria and other exotic diseases. When he got there, he found that the drug he was prescribing most was Prozac! Even in this tiny village in Africa, stress was the #1 problem.

Dr. Weil's story really hit home. It helped me realize that everybody experiences stress. It doesn't matter where you live, what society you live in, what your economic level is, or even how old you are. A baby who is hungry is stressed. A farmer in a small African village who loses his cow is stressed. Someone who has an overbearing boss is stressed. From the day you are born till the day you die, you are going to have stress.

I'm a practical person. If there is no way we can avoid stress, it's up to us to learn how to deal with it. I think that is vitally important for our health. And we should avoid taking medication if we can help it. There are things we can do ourselves, naturally, with just our bodies and minds. That was my attraction to OASIS.

When I was in the OASIS Training, I realized that I already used some of the techniques in my Personal Fitness work: things like using your breath, stretching your body consciously. But learning how to teach the techniques to others in the short and sweet OASIS way helped me internalize them even more myself. And this in turn made my teaching of them more useful for my clients—and my family!

The Cue-2-Do technique was very useful with my children. At the time they were 14, 12, 10, and 8 years old. One of the things about having kids so close in age is that they aggravate each other. My second oldest child is a master at getting people to react. When he was about ten, he told me that he knew a fact about himself: "I am an aggravator. That is my skill. I intend to get better at it." And he did! Getting him to stop aggravating his siblings was difficult. And it was only one part of the equation. Dealing with his "skill" was a challenge for me, and also a growing lesson for the other kids.

I taught them how to "change the channel," not just with their brother, but any time someone would bug them. I reminded my children that in life, you can't always choose the people you have to be around. They might have a personality conflict with someone in their class, or their family, or later they may have a boss they don't get along with. Cue-2-Do taught my children how to tune someone out and switch to an attitude that is more useful.

I used the technique myself a lot, especially when I was dealing with all the challenges with my larger family when my mother was dying. I would ask myself: what's really important right now? Then I could get off an energy-sucking channel to something more useful. With my kids I call it my "anti-whining technique." With myself, it's often getting off the "poor me" channel and switching to the gratitude channel.

Another OASIS Strategy that seems so simple has surprised me many times with its effectiveness. When I taught my yoga class, I would often take a couple of minutes at the end to do the 1 Stone with my students. I didn't think much about it;

I just did it. Then one day when I was in the grocery store, one of my clients came up to me, pulled out her stone, and told me that for the first time in 20 years, she was not having anxiety attacks. She held out her stone for me to see and said, "I carry it around in my pocket." I was impressed, because I didn't teach her a whole class in OASIS, just a couple of minutes at the end. She had learned 1 Stone three weeks before, and it was having a major impact in her life—no more anxiety attacks.

how do you get rid of cellulite?

IN 2008, OPRAH FEATURED ME as one of the "Thirty-Something Women in America." It was "the job you'd never expect"—I am a Personal Trainer, an orthodox Sunni Muslim and I dress in full Islamic garb. Oprah and I spoke of what life was like for me being a mom, a wife, a Muslim AND a fitness trainer. One of the things that I spoke of in that interview was the common goal of health and fitness for all women. I said: "No matter where you choose to worship, all women want to know the same thing… How do you get rid of cellulite?!"

Over the last few years, in addition to owning a fitness studio, I have hosted health and fitness retreats for women throughout the United States and in Bermuda. After my photo landed on the front page of *The New York Times*, I received an invitation to bring my retreat to The King Abdullah University of Science and Technology in Saudi Arabia. Despite being in a predominately Muslim country, the attendees were very diverse—women from the US, UK and Arab countries that were working and living on the KAUST campus. The experience at KAUST re-emphasized for me that all women have a common goal: the desire to be healthy—the best version of themselves. If my journey as a personal trainer has emphasized anything to me, it would be that fact. The desire to be healthy is universal: it crosses cultural, religious, racial and economic lines.

back home

AS MUCH AS I ENJOYED MY INTERNATIONAL WORK, something else was pulling at my heart. Something about my mother's illness and death pushed me to come back home and do more for the women right here in New Haven.

As I mentioned before, I have worked for 13 years as a professional trainer. I always tailor my work to the specific needs of my clients: what is their lifestyle, their financial level, their family situation. However, I began to realize that the people who needed me most were the people who couldn't afford me. When I ran a "discount special" that ran for several weeks, some women would come and make great progress. But once the special would run out, they didn't have money to pay for my regular rates, so they stopped coming—and they fell back into their old patterns and/or gained the weight back.

About four years ago, some colleagues and I came up with an idea: why not have a health and wellness center right here in New Haven, where people would pay whatever they could afford? We knew about the Yale studies that showed that 71% of people in our targeted neighborhood are overweight or obese, with rates of high blood pressure and diabetes alarmingly higher than the national average. Another study showed that in the K-8 grade range in New Haven schools, 47% of the girls are overweight or obese. This is far above the national average. Another alarming fact, especially since it is shown that when obesity begins early in life, the chances of developing diabetes, high blood pressure and other diseases increase astronomically.

My colleagues and I knew that if we could reverse—and even prevent—these diseases, by helping people adopt a different lifestyle, we could help these populations be healthier. My mother developed gestational diabetes when she was pregnant with my sister, and became insulin dependent shortly after that. It is an outrage that she had diabetes for 25 years, and not one doctor—not one person—sent her to a dietitian, a nutritionist, or anyone who could teach her how to manage her health and her stress!

We dreamed up *Fit Haven,* a health and fitness center open to all women and girls, regardless of their age or income. Our vision is to *educate* people so that they know how to take care of their health, and to "reduce health disparity among women in New Haven through physical fitness, nutrition education, and stress management." Stress *management*, rather than stress *prevention*, will be a major part of our program, because stress affects every part of health. When a woman comes to us to lose weight, we will not just talk diet or do physical fitness with her; we will educate her. We will let her know facts about how stress affects her weight and her health. Studies show that when you are stressed, you often lose sleep. When you lose sleep, or your sleep is disrupted, your insulin level rises, and there is an increase in ghrelin, the hormones that tell you that you are hungry, so you eat more, and a decrease in leptin, the hormone that tells you to stop eating. So weight gain becomes a part of the cycle. When a woman understands these facts and is learning practices that can help her put them in their daily life, she has a chance to break the cycle on a lasting basis.

Our dream is becoming a reality. *Fit Haven* is now an established 501(c)(3) organization. We have received major grants from Walmart, Stop and Shop, Regional Water Authority, Graustein Memorial Fund, and Yale-New Haven Hospital, created a partnership with Clifford Beers Clinic, and galvanized support from Mayor Toni Harp, State Senator Gary Winfield, The Housing Authority of New Haven, and from many individuals who believe in the importance of our work. We are now in negotiation for a beautiful space in the Dixwell-Newhallville neighborhood, our desired target area.

We will be the first health and fitness center in Connecticut for women and girls only. We know that if we change the way the woman in the house thinks about shopping, cooking, what she packs in her kid's lunches, how she takes care of her total health—physical, emotional, and spiritual—this will affect generations.

My mother stirred my passion and inspired this dream. Not just her difficulties, but the strength and resourcefulness with which she raised me and my five siblings by herself, and managed to give so much to her community in spite of everything. I know she would be very happy to know that her daughter is helping women in our community get healthier and happier.

HOWARD REYES, MSW, LCSW, is the first full-time Clinical Social Worker assigned to the newly formed Warrior Transition Battalion at Schofield Barracks, Hawaii. As the former Pacific Regional Medical Command Supervisor for the Care Provider Support Program, he supported and enhanced the resiliency of US Army health care providers and staff throughout the Pacific Region.

Howard has worked for over nine years for Tripler Army Medical Center, Hawaii. He has advanced training in Cognitive Therapy, EMDR, and Therapeutic Enactment for trauma treatment, and is co-author of publications for the Hawaii State Legislature and *Crime, Law & Social Change*.

e-mail: howard.l.reyes.civ@mail.mil

millie and me and the us army

THIS IS THE STORY OF HOW A CHANCE ENCOUNTER at a long-ago conference in Phoenix, Arizona turned into sowing the seeds of OASIS across the globe, anywhere the US Army has hospitals and clinics.

I first met Millie Grenough at the 2008 Annual Conference of the EMDR (Eye Movement Desensitization & Reprocessing) International Association in Phoenix. The folks at this conference, psychotherapists working with people who had experienced severe trauma, were brimming with energy and enthusiasm for the work that we do. We were inspired and receptive to the sharing of new ideas and therapy strategies. From a plethora of presentations, I chose to see Millie's. Something about her colorful way of describing herself and her talking points in the program-guide resonated with me.

On the first morning of the conference, when it was not yet 7 AM Hawaii Standard Time on my home island of Oahu, I found myself doing my first OASIS Strategy, the 4-D. At the outset, I did it just to humor this very nice lady presenter, but the exercise worked its own minor miracle of rousing me without a drop of Starbucks. But what truly piqued my interest were her stories—her adventures as a nun in South America, the suspense of her fateful bike ride, and all of the wonderful pictures she painted of a life lived with spiritual strength, fearlessness, and the deepest love of humanity.

A few years later, I took on the Program Supervisor's job in the Pacific Regional Medical Command's Care Provider Support Program (CPSP). In 2012 when we organized our annual conference for US Army Medical Providers and Resiliency Trainers worldwide, we chose *Trauma and Mindfulness* as our overall theme. It seemed the perfect opportunity to invite Millie to be one of the principal trainers.

Trauma is certainly something that we have to deal with on a minute-to-minute basis, whether it is on the battlefield with military on active duty, in hospitals with the wounded, or working with the families and our own colleagues. In situations where we, as care providers, are under constant pressure to deal with such severe trauma, mindfulness is often hard to come by.

So Millie came to spend two days with us, just outside Ft. Sam Houston in San Antonio. Thirty-five of us Care Providers flew in from all over—Afghanistan, Germany, Hawaii, Iraq, Korea, and multiple Army Medical Centers on the US Mainland. We were ready to dive into best practices for dealing with trauma and, if possible, initiate our own practice of mindfulness—a tall order for seasoned US Army Soldiers and Civilians. We Army folks are excellent at taking fast action in dealing with other people's emergencies, but not so skilled at taking care of ourselves with gentle calmness.

Somewhat to our surprise, we had about the most fun a group can have in learning new skills and strategies. In the beginning we were reluctant to lead the OASIS Strategies ourselves. But after some practice in small groups, we loosened up, and began to experiment and have fun with different ways of doing the Strategies that suited our personalities and our particular work situations. We came up with new phrases: the 3-B-C became "tactical breathing," mindfulness morphed into "situational awareness." Since we never know what's going to face us, we always need to be flexible and resilient. We started referring to ourselves as the Resiliency Police, with the motto *Semper Fi & Semper Gumpy.*

Evaluations after the training included words such as "content," "calm," "peaceful," "happy," "excited," "giddy," "clear," "enlightened," "relaxed." These words were not from a list of words provided; they came unsolicited.

after giddiness, what?

OUR ENTHUSIASM AND LEARNING WERE CLEAR in San Antonio. Now, back on our bases and in our hospitals, how could we keep that energy and bring what we experienced into our mission? How to keep our mindful presence to support and enhance the resiliency of US Army health-care providers and staff throughout the Pacific Region? I had the benefit of working with my colleague Richard Ries, Psy.D, who had also been a key part of our San Antonio conference, so we were able to remind each other to walk our talk. This meant, among other things, remembering to do the OASIS Strategies ourselves.

Dr. Ries and I designed a program to bring these *Trauma and Mindfulness* strategies to our hard-working colleagues in the Pacific Region—and our efforts paid off. In 2013, our CSPS Program garnered American Psychological Association (APA) recognition as one of four *"Best Practice"* winners nationwide. Our program was lauded by the APA's *Psychologically Healthy Workplace Awards,* the *Pacific Business News,* the *Army Times,* and the US Army homepage. We were especially praised for helping to create "a psychologically healthy workplace that promotes an organizational culture that values well-being and performance and delivers results on both sides of the equation." OASIS Strategies and mindfulness did their job. Richard Ries and I celebrated with our colleagues, Tripler Army Medical Center and CPSP were recognized at a ceremony in Washington DC, and our hospital was awarded a permanent plaque.

life goes on

THE NEXT TIME I SPOKE WITH MILLIE was about six months after receiving our award. At the time of the call I faced the dual overwhelm of our CPSP program being eviscerated by the Army Medical Command, due to funding cuts, and the fact that I would need to do a lot of scrambling in order to even have another position once our funding was eliminated. I remember driving down the H-1 freeway into work, calling Millie in Connecticut, and describing this chaotic mess to Millie. She unceremoniously invited me to do a 3-B-C-type breathing exercise right there in my vehicle. I was not able to "rest both hands gently on my belly" as I was heading down a hill at about 67 miles per hour... Needless to say, Millie drove home some strong messages. Not only did I need to pause in my own state of overwhelm and take care of myself, but we really CAN do this anytime and anywhere, if we take just one minute.

From the Warrior Transition Battalion at Schofield Barracks in Hawaii, thank you, Millie—for sharing a lifetime's worth of your *mana* (Hawaiian for "wisdom") and for being such a good friend to so many of us.

 **ANN REEVES,** is a psychologist and Authorized OASIS Facilitator who works with folks of all ages in her private practice in Connecticut. She specializes in psychotherapy and mindfulness-based stress reduction, blending traditional psychotherapy with alternative techniques, because of the evidence that mind-body therapies can enhance psychological healing.

Ann: "We are each a whole person, not just a mind. I especially celebrate the healing gifts of the natural world by conducting workshops in beautiful settings, where we deepen our awareness, feel more peaceful, and transform stress through re-connecting with the elements of earth, wind, water, and fire."

e-mail: acreeves@optonline.net

learning to surf

THE SMALL BLUE BOOK CALLED OUT TO ME from the registration table at a therapeutic training seminar: *OASIS in the Overwhelm: 60-second strategies for balance in a busy world*, by a Millie Grenough. The cover looked so peaceful, with colors representing sand, water, and sky, and a palm tree instead of the "I" in "OASIS," transporting me instantly to memories of a relaxing summer spent in Maui.

There was an endorsement by Bernie Siegel, a recognized expert in the field of complementary medicine and one of my heroes. My eyes fell on the sentence, "You can't stop the waves, but you can learn to surf"—a quote from Jon Kabat-Zinn, founder of the Mindfulness-Based Stress Reduction Clinic at the University of Massachusetts Medical School. He is another thinker I deeply admire. A recent internship at his clinic, as part of my ongoing studies of alternative forms of healing and spiritual expression, had further developed my understanding of the detrimental effects of stress, and how the mindfulness perspective he has developed can help us manage and reduce stress.

So much intrigued me in this little blue book, both personally and professionally. "Ahh," I wondered, "Balance in 60 seconds? Is that even possible?" Both attracted and skeptical, I bought the book and started reading.

I work as a psychotherapist with children and adults who struggle with anxiety or problems of everyday living. Many of the children I see also present with significant behavioral difficulties. In addition, I teach stress transformation work-shops. Having been educated in psychodynamic theory in graduate school, I had also discovered the benefits of adding cognitive behavioral theory and techniques as a practical and effective means for working with many psychological problems, especially anxiety. I had learned that what we think about a situation or personal experience has a profound influence on how we feel about it, and that the point of transformation may come about through our shifting habitual ways of thinking, thereby changing one's feelings and subsequent behavior.

So while little content in this book was new to me, Millie Grenough's brilliance was to synthesize in easy-to-understand terms such practices and concepts as brain neuro-plasticity, the nature of the physiological and psychological connection of mind and body, cognitive restructuring, and meditation. She simplified and packaged them into "a delivery system" so that others would have ready access to four well-tried techniques for defusing stress. And they really do take only one minute each! This approach seemed the perfect com-panion to much of what I had learned and tried to incorporate into my own life.

I have been told that I bring enthusiasm, curiosity, intuition, and compassion to the table. I have a youthful soul, and wide-ranging experiences in travel and with people of other cultures that inspire and motivate me. I also struggle mightily with organization, time management, procrastination, prioritizing, and other aspects of what is called executive function. From another perspective, I might be described as a seeker, with a deep connection to the natural and spiritual world, someone with exposure and training in many alternative healing modalities and ways of looking at the world. These two aspects of myself don't always mesh together. Learning to say "no" is a lifelong assignment, as I simply want to do it all, and am often overwhelmed with too many interests and commitments.

Although I did not act right away, I never forgot Millie and her book, and when the time was right, I recognized a personal and professional opportunity to enhance my skills. I signed up for the OASIS Training to become an Authorized OASIS Facilitator.

The training offered genuine hospitality and goodwill among the interesting and enthusiastic participants. And we were soon able to experience the deep effect of these deceptively simple exercises.

The OASIS Strategies clicked with the many cognitive behavioral interventions I had studied, and had used with my clients. The Cue-2-Do is effective at helping someone break out of a habitual emotional response or sustained negative mood by challenging the thinking process.

And while the three breaths of the 3-B-C may not seem to have a long-term effect on our mental health status, those three breaths will help you deal with the guy who cuts you off on your way home from work—or prevent you from saying something you will later regret when someone has let you down. And just maybe a day, and then two days, and then a month of three breaths at a time will begin to make a real difference. Just getting your body to move (4-D) can get your energy flowing again and make it easier to concentrate on the task at hand. The 1 Stone exercise helps folks to focus on the here and now. It helps us to slow down and notice things we might never otherwise see. This exercise quiets the mind, calms the emotions, enhances awareness, and creates physiological changes in the body, such as shutting down the flooding of "worry juice" (cortisol), the stress hormone that can flood our bodies.

I have used the OASIS Strategies in a variety of ways, both in my private practice of psychotherapy and in a series of workshops/retreats that I have designed. Several of my clients have benefited greatly from these techniques.

stephen

STEPHEN IS A NINE-YEAR-OLD BOY who can be warm and very kind, but who also harbors considerable anxieties. He lives within a loving family with several siblings and mature, psychologically sophisticated parents. In school, Stephen exhibits model behavior. He cares very much what people think of him and would never dare to bend the rules. At home, he is quite the opposite. He is whiny, demanding attention at impractical moments. Stephen has serious meltdowns, where he can go "from 0 to 80" in a few seconds. During those episodes it is impossible to reach him, and he is unable to see reason or put things in perspective. When we discuss these episodes in our sessions, he often can't remember the specifics.

Stephen yearns for more harmonious relationships within his family. He feels guilty about his behavior, which in turn lowers his self-esteem. Although his behavior may look "spoiled" when he doesn't get his way, it is actually brought on by his fear of dealing with anything unexpected. Stephen worries intensely about what's going to happen in the future. This anticipatory anxiety leads to an acute need to control all aspects of his life. The energy this process takes is considerable, and keeps Stephen from enjoying his childhood.

Along with progressive muscle relaxation, I taught Stephen several of the OASIS Strategies. The 4-D exercise has helped dispel some of his considerable physical energy, so that he can be more available to therapy. The 3-B-C strategy was particularly useful, because he can do the deep belly breathing without calling attention to himself, such as in the classroom. The 1 Stone exercise has helped him manage his anticipatory anxiety. It teaches him how to look carefully and mindfully at one thing or idea in the present, instead of reflecting back on something that has already happened or worrying about something that is coming up in the future.

Lastly, I recognized that the key for him was recognizing the "early warning system" or cues to his discomfort before a meltdown. The Cue-2-Do technique does just that. Stephen is learning to identify stressed or anxious feelings earlier, so that he might realize that there is not much he can do about the current situation or, more accurately, that he has again fallen into habitual patterns of thinking ("I need to have what I think I want in order to feel more in control") or feeling (that is, being frustrated and angry). At such times, he is learning that he has options, such as "changing the channel" to a positive one. His positive channels include focusing on something he is looking forward to, or a memory of a happy experience in his life when he felt relaxed and successful, such as a soccer game or a playdate with a friend.

christine

CHRISTINE IS A WARM, CREATIVE ELEVEN-YEAR-OLD middle school student. Intuitive and highly sensitive, she possesses unusually mature psychological insight into other people, but not always into herself. Christine also struggles with a dual diagnosis of attention-deficit hyperactivity disorder and a severe obsessive-compulsive disorder, having difficulty maintaining personal boundaries and managing intrusive, frightening thoughts. Christine works very hard and courageously in psychotherapy and often puts into practice the many techniques she has learned, especially in school. She is philosophical about her psychological status and endeavors to overcome specific symptoms as they arise, recognizing them as just that—symptoms.

Christine is never afraid to ask for assistance, whether in school, at home, or in my office, to alleviate her symptoms. Our work together often involves grounding and movement exercises, among them the 4-D, which gives her an opportunity to stretch and energize her body and feel more physiologically organized. Christine has long used breath control to calm herself down, so the 3-B-C works well for her. She can use it preventively, or she can use the Emergency 3-B-C when she is faced with acute anxiety in the moment.

As Christine has a fertile imagination, she has enjoyed taking the Mini-Vacation (Personal Palm Pilot) 3-B-C, which allows her to calm herself through visualizing a safe and beautiful vacation spot. She is able to see, hear, and feel the environment, such as a warm breeze on her face, or a beach or tall tree, and can "see" trusted others with her. By rubbing her hands together briskly and placing them over her eyes while she breathes deeply during this visualization, she is enhancing her experience, as hands are transmitters and receptors of energy.

Christine also has profited from guided visualization and meditation, and has experienced healing thoughts and images during such times. For this reason I have taught her the Here-and-Now Preventive 3-B-C, to help her stay calm when she gets anxious about something coming up. On one occasion, she gazed around the room until she noted a beautiful verdigris vase she thought was beautiful. As she continued to gaze at the blue-green-copper patina, she invited the color, texture, and graceful form into herself, while she slowly breathed three times. Christine also enjoys the 1 Stone strategy where she chooses a stone and examines it closely, being one with it while breathing slowly ten times.

Lastly, we have utilized the Cue-2-Do strategy, as Christine is so perceptive and intuitive. We spoke about the reflex elicited when her pediatrician strikes her knee with a rubber hammer during a routine examination. I called this a "knee-jerk reaction," and noted that we often have emotional knee-jerk reactions when faced with a stressful situation. Using the concept of changing TV channels, I taught Christine that when she finds she is stuck on one knee-jerk reaction or feeling channel (for her, it is crippling anxiety) she can evaluate the situation by tuning in to her body and asking five questions. She now realizes that she can make the choice to simply change the feeling channel to "confident" or "relaxed," using her imaginary remote.

It is inspiring to see a young courageous person profit in the face of her day-to-day challenges from such deceptively simple, yet highly effective strategies. With children, we can rehearse such scenarios over and over in role-play, often writing them down as scripts, sometimes with pictures. This is similar to the social stories approach of helping a child modify her/his behavior.

elements of nature

I HAVE DEVELOPED A WORKSHOP/RETREAT entitled *Earth, Wind, Water, Fire: Re-Connecting with the Earth Through the Element of Nature* or *Transforming Stress through the Elements of Nature*, depending on the group's needs. I see stress as a form of energy, and the study of physics tells us that energy cannot be destroyed, only transformed. With growing research on the importance of nature to our mental and physical health, we dwell on the nature and celebration of the elements, and the use of nature for stress transformation.

On a recent summer day, nine of us met in a cabin at a rustic, forested farm and retreat center with ponds, hiking trails, flowers, and a feeling of utter peace. We each shared early memories of our relationship with nature and discussed our perceptions of each element, focusing on what we might learn from them. Then we spent time alone outdoors, discovering our own relationship with that element and performing healing rituals that honored our relationship.

OASIS Strategies were integrated into the Wind, Water, and Fire segments. While Earth focuses on grounding exercises and regeneration, the lessons from Wind are breathing and movement, a perfect opportunity to incorporate the 3-B-C breathing exercises and the 4-D movement strategies facing the north, south, east, and west.

The element of Water teaches us about depth, whether dreaming, or the unconscious. This is a fortuitous opportunity to work with meditation, including the 1 Stone strategy that Thich Nhat Hanh used so effectively with children, holding, examining, and focusing on a stone in their hands.

The last element, Fire, is about passion and creativity, both that of the earth and our own. Retreatants were encouraged to think about their own dreams and passions and to what extent they felt separated from them, either by life circumstances or by a blocking belief.

We talked about stress and strong emotions, both positive and negative. This seemed a perfect time to teach the Cue-2-Do technique, using the five steps to learn how to change from rigid patterns of thinking to increased options by changing the emotional channel we were on. In relationship to Fire, it gave us an opportunity to inspire our passions and forge new ideas and beliefs, whenever we found that we were limiting ourselves by self-imposed emotional knee-jerk reactions.

community

THE "O" IN OASIS IS A CIRCLE. The archetype of a circle conveys inclusivity and community. As the shape of OASIS was formed and the original book was published, it was Millie's desire to contribute to the common good, by sharing the techniques that she had developed with like-minded persons. Thus the OASIS Community was born, a diverse group of individuals who, like me, appreciate the significance of her work. Millie's contributions are not limited to four 60-second techniques. Rather, she folds these strategies into highly nuanced, population-specific presentations on a variety of topics. She encourages us in the OASIS Community to do the same. We are free to fold her strategies into our own ways of working, tailored to the communities we serve. Several times a year the Authorized OASIS Facilitators gather to compare notes and share new techniques. Such occasions serve as community touchstones for inspiration and renewal.

learning to surf

IN MY LIFE, THE WAVES CONTINUE TO ROLL IN minute-by-minute and day-by-day. Often they are gentle and low, but sometimes they are ferocious, easily leading to the precipice of overwhelm. For me, the most difficult aspect of the OASIS 60-second techniques is remembering to do them at all! Sometimes, when the waves appear particularly daunting, I need to be reminded by others to use them. Like anything else in life, learning does take a certain amount of self-discipline and practice, and the more I have practiced these skills, the more automatic they have become. Teaching helps to inspire me to keep on keeping on.

So, do I ever feel overwhelmed? You bet. But I am learning to surf, and my skills are no longer at the beginner's level. This can happen for anyone. For everyone. Especially you.

JILL BERQUIST, founder of *Berquist Coaching Services*, is an Executive Coach helping leaders tap their unique brilliance to live with greater purpose, inspiration and impact. Jill's high-performing clients are seeking a way to enhance their game, while regaining greater energy, passion, connection, and peace. Jill has also helped hundreds of clients with successful transitions, applying their unique gifts for greater freedom and fulfillment.

In 2000, Jill earned her Professional Certified Coach (PCC) accreditation through the International Coach Federation. In 2005, Jill was an OASIS Pioneer Facilitator of the OASIS Strategies. She is co-author of *OASIS in the Overwhelm 28 Day Guide: Rewire Your Brain from Chaos to Calm* (2007).

e-mail: jill@berquistcoaching.com
website: www.berquistcoaching.com

a versatile intervention

my path to oasis

TWENTY-FIVE YEARS AGO, long before burnout was as common-place or publicized as it is today, I was Director of Recruiting for a global professional services firm. The organization prided itself on its "work hard—play hard" culture that attracted only the best and brightest. Yet, there were two issues. The time the consultants spent working hard far exceeded any time they spent playing. Public chats about stress, and the sharing of strategies for dealing with it, were basically nonexistent.

Seventeen years ago I started my own business, coaching similar high performers. I wanted to help my clients achieve their career goals, but not at the price of sacrificing their health or their souls in the quest for "success." Viewing stress management and self-care as essential ingredients in our work, I used various tools of my own to address this piece of their personal development.

In 2006, I first heard Millie Grenough share her incredible story of healing from a near-death bike accident. Millie exuded a graceful yet penetrating sense of confidence and calm, and I found the OASIS tactics highly intriguing. The strategies resonated with me for a number of reasons. They were:

- elegantly simple; they could be taught clearly, learned quickly and applied immediately;

- based on neuroscience principles and what we know about how the brain responds to stress; and

- could change the way we habitually respond to stress, so that we can make conscious, healthy choices about how we manage our stress.

The principle of neuroplasticity shows that our brains are forming new neurons all the time. No matter how long a habit is in place, with practice new neural pathways can be formed and new habits can take hold. "With practice" is the operative phrase. Old habits die hard, yet it can be done. Aha! This is where OASIS offers an important link that's missing from most other approaches. Other strategies may seem slick, but if they're not simple and direct, we won't use them regularly. They won't create a real shift in our behavior. But the short and effective 60-second OASIS Strategies offer a real shot at change!

I wanted this benefit for my clients and for me, so I jumped right into the OASIS Pioneer Facilitator group. A year later, when Millie asked if I would co-author the *OASIS 28 Day Guide*, I was happy to. Aside from using the tools with clients and family, I was happy to have another way to share the important work of OASIS with the world.

it's personal

AT THE TIME I WAS PLANNING to begin my OASIS journey, my mother was planning her move from Maryland to Connecticut to be closer to my family. Given my mother's "difficult" personality and our family history, what for some could be a time of celebration, for me was a time for safeguarding. Although I typically err on the side of optimism, I knew this event could be incredibly challenging. My mother's move would bring a strong test on my boundaries, patience and resolve. Bracing myself with some new stress management tactics could only be a good thing. The proactive gal that I am, I secured a counselor, was watching my healthy habits, and now—I added OASIS to the plan.

Despite some happy moments with family and grandchildren, the baseline of my mom's demeanor was "prickly," and her demands and criticism had a way of easily pushing my buttons. The breathing and meditation strategies were helpful to protect myself. River stones were placed around my home, office, and even my car, as a reminder for me to slow down, breathe deeply, and pull myself back to center. The OASIS Strategies enabled me to be more respectful and positive— what I truly wanted to model for my kids.

Speaking of my children, OASIS comes in handy with my two "spirited" (a.k.a high-drama) daughters. I recall a classic moment when my then-five-year-old was having a meltdown—about what, I have no recollection. I do remember her wailing her little lungs out in full tantrum at the top of stairs, looking down at me. I went to her, sharing hugs and what I was convinced would be words of calm and encouragement, but nothing was working. It was time to call in an OASIS Strategy, the 4-D or "Four Directions." I promptly asked my daughter to shout her four favorite foods as we stretched together in all directions, one reach and breath at a time. A round of gummy bears, pizza and ice cream later, our crisis was averted. This is only one example of many.

The funny thing is that over the past eight years since, when my daughters see me getting emotional or on the verge of an eruption, they're happy to throw it back in my face. They take their own inhale and exhale, with a smirk, saying, "Just breathe, Mom." If they are being especially fresh, they will throw in an "Ommmm" for good measure.

anywhere, anytime, any way

I ENJOY SHARING the OASIS Strategies with diverse groups, from attorneys, entrepreneurs and project managers to stay-at-home moms, executives and Brownie Troops. Participants especially enjoy the demonstration of exactly how to use the techniques. It's really the best part. They learn something practical they can apply in their lives, while experiencing an immediate dose of peace.

One time, at a regional conference for a national childcare organization, I was slated to do an OASIS Training with three groups of about 30 teachers each. Traditionally, the 1 Stone open-eye meditation is taught with a river stone or something else from nature. I've done it using beach shells or beach stones. The day of the conference I had forgotten my box of river stones. When I realized this, I quickly looked around for a substitute. Since we were in a hotel breakout room, each place setting had a water glass, a pen and a hard candy. I asked each teacher to hold the candy in the palm of his or her hand. We walked through the ten slow breaths in and out, while keeping our relaxed attention on our meditation object. We had just changed the OASIS 1 Stone to the 1 Candy. It may not have been as ideal as a river stone or other natural object, but it did the trick.

I love the flexibility of the OASIS Strategies. You never know the exact moment you'll need to call upon a stress management tool, and OASIS methods are always in your proverbial "hip pocket."

small changes, big results

IN THE WORLD OF THE INTENSE, "TYPE-A" EXECUTIVE, there's often an apparent void when it comes to emotion management skills. Some executives are not even aware they are functioning in a chronic state of high stress. These "drivers" are used to tolerating and pushing through. They don't see how this stress could be affecting their relationships, work and health. Although that happens to so many of us, for this group, it is harder. The demands these leaders put on themselves, layered with the expectations others put on them, suck them into a perpetual vortex of vise-grip tension. This level of tension can have a far-reaching and dire impact. Yet, when mastered, effective approaches to contend with stress have a pervasive and far-reaching *positive* impact.

We know from research that the ability to manage stress positively impacts blood pressure, digestion, immunity, sleep, and many other health factors. It can diminish mood swings, and increase optimism, sense of peace and overall well-being. It also builds confidence when the world is swirling around us, as it often is for the busy executive. Knowing how to tame our stress can help us gain access to the ever-elusive sense of control.

Studies also tell us that stress management directly impacts emotional intelligence, a core attribute that makes for great leaders. As someone does better with self-control, they can think before reacting, convey greater empathy and build more successful relationships. Leaders can create colossal change through addressing emotion regulation and management. Often, working with a coach on their professional and personal development, for the first time they can slow down long enough to look beneath the good warrior mask they're wearing. And although this may be challenging, it can be the start of a transformation they never imagined, as the following story illustrates.

I was recently engaged to assist a VP of Operations with emotion regulation, communication and life/work balance, at a critical time in his career and for his company. Changing his name to maintain confidentiality, we'll call him Tom. Tom is super-bright, highly respected for his knowledge and drive, and usually a very likable, good-humored guy. In fact, he can be a real character. Tom was juggling the oversight of day-to-day operations for one plant, overseeing operations at four others, and he had just acquired oversight of two more. The stress of Tom's job, already huge, had become enormous. When he had things under control, he was as charismatic and inspiring as the best of them. But lately, under long stretches of duress, and with certain triggers, Tom sometimes lost patience, used a terse edge in his communication, or even blew up. It was crucial for Tom to deal with anger and stress management, to remove what could become an obstacle to his highest potential and happiness.

We began with stress-management strategies. Early on we introduced slow, deep breathing. A unique factor about this client, and why something as basic as breathing had such a big impact in helping him with stress, had to do with his athletic background. To Tom, the concept of deep breathing was really new. Tom had been a high-ranked competitive swimmer almost his entire life. He had been on his high school and college swim teams and he coached the town league. Today, Tom continues to swim for fitness and in various triathlons. He told me that as a swimmer, he spent his life holding his breath! He boasted that the way he cleans his pool is manually—holding his breath and swimming under water with the hose.

We identified some trigger events that would easily create a knee-jerk reaction of stress. We focused primarily on some slow, deep breathing when these triggers occurred, to gain composure, and to think before responding. I would get emails with updates: "Coach, after receiving this very disturbing email from Bill, I am not responding right away. I am breathing." In fact, when Tom was having a brutal day, I would sometimes get a text: "Good day for breathing."

Through the 360-degree feedback survey I conducted at the end of the engagement, multiple comments mentioned that Tom is now much more thoughtful when dealing with high-pressure situations. Input says he is pausing and responding consciously, and his newer strategies are creating a very different image for him. He is personally feeling in greater control of his emotions and moods, and this has rippled out to the quality of his professional and personal relationships. It appears that breathing in—*and out*, for that matter—has been an effective strategy in creating his pretty positive results.

one size doesn't fit all

THE OASIS TECHNIQUES ARE COMPLETELY CUSTOMIZABLE to various situations and to each person's needs. For example, breathing and slowing down makes a huge impact for some, while others may need a variety of strategies and options. A method that works at home might be inappropriate or awkward during a business meeting. But there are always ways to modify the technique so it will still work.

I receive great joy from helping others gain greater calm and control in their lives, even if we start one moment at a time. Eventually the moments string together, and a personal evolution is possible. My hope for you, and all of us, is that we just stay on that path of peace. I know for sure life will keep serving up tests for our techniques. And with a little luck (and a bit of practice), we'll keep rising to the challenge.

To our unique OASIS journeys...!

GEORGE HERRICK is an Authorized OASIS Facilitator and Certified Master Life Coach, specializing in advanced recovery from addiction. "Part of what I love about OASIS in the Overwhelm is how it provides simple, easy tools, catalysts for growth and transformation."

George is initiated in Incan shamanic practices, and is the co-creator of *The Wilderness Walk*, a deep experiential process that guides participants to accept, respect and learn from uncomfortable emotions such as pain, fear, sadness and anger.

e-mail: georgeherrick@sbcglobal.net
website: www.georgeherrick.com

oasis in recovery

FRANK WAS OVERWHELMED. A recently singled parent, he sat slumped in my office with the weight of his world on his shoulders.

He wasn't single by choice. His wife of 23 years, whom he had met by chance at the base of a waterfall on a trail in Colorado, had died six months earlier after a long, eroding journey through the shadowy canyons of cancer. He now had two girls in prestigious universities, each with only partial scholarships. Prestige is pricey, but "their dreams are not disposable," he liked to say.

And here he sat, an essentially vital, youthful, energetic, athletic man, looking old for the first time since he came to see me when his wife's life began to ebb. Years earlier, he had overcome the demons of addiction. I wondered if his addiction was calling him back.

"It's all gone, George, I'm lost at sea." I asked him what happened. His job as a senior executive at a major insurance firm had just been "de-contracted," a term I hadn't heard before but clearly was a euphemism for being fired.

Frank began to paint the picture he needed me to see. While he was given a fair, competitive severance package, the burden of his debt from his wife's long illness and his girls' education felt as if it were beyond the scope of his resources. I had guessed rightly that his over-the-top stress level was triggering thoughts of relapse. "I just want to say screw it and get wasted! This is just too damn much on top of losing Sharon."

At times like this, when life feels complicated and all twisted in knots, my coaching clients tend to want some complex trick of the trade that matches the convolutions of their thinking. Frank was no exception. But instead, I offered him something exquisitely simple. I asked him to put both hands on his abdomen and exhale deeply. He balked a little, but went along. I told him to relax a little as his breath flowed out, completely emptying his lungs. I suggested he inhale naturally through his nose, with no thought, effort or control, deep into his belly and chest, completely filling his torso. Then I had him repeat the process two more times.

"How do you feel in this instant?" I asked. He started to go back into the story of all that had happened, but I put my hand up and stopped him. "How do you feel in this instant?" I repeated. "OK, but—" he began. I interrupted and repeated the question a third time. He acknowledged he was feeling more relaxed. I asked him from which energetic place he thought he had a better chance of thinking about solutions, this state or how he felt when he arrived a half hour earlier. "This is better, much better," he responded. Frank has been a 3-B-C advocate ever since. (And has added 4-D, Cue-2-Do and 1 Stone to his repertoire!)

Many people in long-term recovery from addictions react to stress on deeper levels than the general public, for a number of reasons. First, stress releases certain chemicals in the brain, among them cortisol, dopamine, norepinephrine and epinephrine. Many of these chemicals are also released in substance use.

They stimulate a variety of reactions: emotional responses to stimuli, excitement, arousal and a heightened sense of urgency. In people with addiction, these natural responses to stress are very likely to trigger a relapse. In addition, some of the chemicals mentioned reduce inhibition and rational thought, and activate long-term memory. This way they cause old memories of stressful situations to get lumped together with the current stressor. Now add to this the fact that people afflicted with addiction, even in recovery, often have poorly developed neuro-programming for coping responses to stress. In other words: they are more prone to stress, but have less ability to deal with stress.

All these factors can create a perfect storm for relapse. When the recovering person is caught unaware in this situation, even normal stress can have potentially devastating consequences. For the person in recovery, all this of course adds another level of stress to an already difficult situation. How true the old joke is, that "addicted people are just like everyone else, only more so!"

Taking a deeper look at how this works, the human body reacts to stress by releasing two types of chemical messengers—hormones in the blood and neurotransmitters in the brain. The hormones alter the body's metabolism in order to ready the body for reactivity such as fight or flight. The neurotransmitters trigger emotional responses such as aggression or anxiety in order to prompt people to take such action.

Substance use alters and inhibits the natural cycle of this chemical release, necessary to respond to stress. However, the stressor itself is still present—all that is missing is a healthy response to it. For example, let's say the addicted person's mortgage is due, but he or she doesn't have enough money to cover it. That would be a major stressor for anyone. But an addict will often use his or her substance to avoid the discomfort of stress. So in this case, rather than respond to the problem, the addict self-medicates with a substance. This goes on for a period of time because withdrawal or detox is itself a stressor, thus exacerbating the crisis in the addict's mind—which (s)he responds to by continuing the substance abuse. The problem grows as the mortgage remains unpaid, with added late fees and interest, and the stress levels increase while the ability to deal with stress decreases.

Research by Dr. Mary Jeanne Kreek at Rockefeller University and by other experts in the field has shown that when the addict halts the substance use and begins sobriety, the acquired hypersensitivity to stress and inability to cope continue, often for long periods. The hormones and neurotransmitters have "learned" a certain response pattern to stress, and must be retaught over time to respond in a healthy, natural pattern. Thus the addict can remain more susceptible to stress yet less equipped to manage it well into sobriety, which makes the risk of relapse a constant concern.

Understanding the effects of stress (specifically, distress) is increasingly important in today's rapid-fire, multitasking, instant-gratification world, as stress has become endemic to our culture. Reasons why it is essential to have strategies to counteract stress include:

1. Untreated stress can lead to illness, which of course adds more stress.

2. Stress can reduce thought function and mindful attention in ways that can increase the risk of accident, also adding more stress.

3. Stress can trigger some of the same brain chemicals that are released in active addiction, tricking the mind into cravings.

4. Stress can lead to emotional reactions such as fear and anger, which are also potential relapse triggers. In fact, the brain's chemical reaction to anger is the same as its reaction to fear. Thus for people in recovery, as we discussed above, normal stress can generate an additional level of stress and thus diminish the recovering person's ability to resolve the original stressor.

recovery tools

THE STRATEGIES OF OASIS IN THE OVERWHELM are perfect tools in recovery because they are:

1. Simple and easy to use (which is critical due to how addiction amplifies stress—so the simpler the tool, the more practical).

2. Memorable.

3. Portable, since no equipment is involved.

4. Easy to incorporate into any recovery model, such as 12-Step or SMART Recovery.

All these factors make the strategies more likely to be used, which increases their effectiveness.

Here is an example of the power and simplicity of OASIS

in the Overwhelm. I was working with a young woman who was in a relatively early stage of recovery. Stacey had been clean from opiate addiction for about two years. She had used drugs to "still the madness," as she put it, as she is type-A and an obsessive, cyclic thinker, what we sometimes call "monkey mind"!

While we worked on some of the underlying reasons for why Stacey was always analyzing, figuring things out, and repeating thoughts over and over, I gave her some simple focusing and grounding tools to practice. Meditation and focusing, for example, were moderately helpful in quieting Stacey's racing thoughts. Her overactive thinking often started in reaction to anxiety and fear, as well as historical emotional pain. She would become ungrounded by her whirling thoughts, and the ensuing chaos opened a real risk of relapse. When I taught her the OASIS Strategy Cue-2-Do, we achieved a real breakthrough. The strategy proved to be a great way to help her bring her energy back down into her body.

Stacey identified some of her particular cues, that is, the physical responses she experienced due to emotional and mental stimuli. She practiced identifying her cues, both their messages in her mind and the corresponding physical sensations in her body, and developed alternative strategies for responding to the cue.

As she practiced, I added the 1 Stone strategy. I knew that for Stacey, having something tangible to hold on to and focus her attention on would expand her capacity to center herself. I gave her a heart-shaped river rock that I had collected long ago, and she used it to grab her attention and shift it from the channel of spinning thoughts to a channel of calm, centered memories of walking by a stream in her childhood. She became able to move from drama to serenity fairly quickly. This combination of OASIS techniques has served her well ever since, and though her thoughts still race at times, she has become skilled at refocusing and slowing the "monkey mind" down.

Stories like this illustrate the amazing power of the brain's neuroplasticity. Neuroplasticity is the ability of the brain to develop throughout life. Science long held that we are born with all the neurons we will ever have, and we use them up or waste them over our lifetime. But current research shows that regardless of our age, we can change our brain and influence how it operates, which can have a direct impact on our health and well-being. New neurons grow throughout our lifespan, and thus we are primed to continue learning. We influence the growth of neurons by what we choose to do and not do. Therefore we could arguably say that *consciousness influences the growth of the organ that generates consciousness!*

Research conducted by Dr. Alvaro Pascual-Leone concluded that where the mind's function is directed, it generates growth, not only in physical practice, but mentally as well. So Mahatma Mohandas Gandhi's famous quotation is not an esoteric platitude, but a literal scientific truth:

Watch your thoughts, for they become words. Watch your words, for they become actions. Watch your actions, for they become habits. Watch your habits, for they become character. Watch your character, for it becomes your destiny.

Added to that, Dr. Jeffrey Schwartz found that adults have the capacity not only to grow new neurons but also to repair damaged ones and change the function of old ones. The power of willful activity shapes the brain function throughout life. Change the willful activity; change the brain! This certainly was true for both Frank and Stacey. As a result they now had new tools augmenting the skills they needed to combat the disease of addiction and sustain their recovery.

The most powerful tools are the simplest, because we stick with them. A tool we don't use is literally useless. We *think* in complexities, but we tend to want to *act* as simply as possible, particularly when learning a new skill. And therein lies the power of the OASIS Strategies. They are simple!

The high level of fear and stress in the world today is having a profound impact on people's physical, mental, emotional and spiritual health. I see the strategies of OASIS as very simple but highly effective tools that actually transform the signs and symptoms of stress, rather than just help the sufferer cope. I am a person in recovery myself, and I have over two decades' experience working with my primary "tribe" of people in long-term recovery who are seeking to rebuild their lives. I can say that the transformational power of OASIS is nowhere more true, nor are the results anywhere more stunning, than in addiction recovery. OASIS in the Overwhelm is a custom fit.

Chief visionary **TANISHA AKINLOYE** is best known for empowering women through her nonprofit organization *Empowering Through Beauty*. She is an entrepreneur, philanthropist, motivational speaker, mindset coach and beauty expert. Her success has led to nationwide recognition within the beauty industry, and support from politicians, colleagues and women leaders.

Tanisha has been featured on Fox Business Network, Modern Salon, *Essence*, *Madame Noire*, and *Connecticut Magazine*, among other media outlets. She was recently recognized and honored by US Senator Chris Murphy, the National Black Professional Women Association and Alpha Kappa Alpha Sorority.

e-mail: info@tanishaakinloye.com
website: www.tanishaakinloye.com

so many reasons

I AM BLESSED WITH the power of forgiveness. Deeply engrained in me by my loving parents, it has allowed me to move through times and experiences of desolation and great pain, determined to learn from these lessons. It has taught me how to heal my wounds, face adversity, and live for tomorrow. It has made me the strong woman I am today. I thank God every day for this blessing, and that he chose me to be a witness of his power.

But even in this great blessing lurks a danger. My ease of forgiving, especially those I love, in the past has caused me to forget, to overlook my pain and numb myself, to blame myself for hurtful experiences, and let myself be soothed back into the same bad situation over and over again.

In 2008, I opened my own beauty salon. At this time in my life I was really challenged by self-doubt and uncertainty, especially after having been a stay-at-home mom for eight years. Because of my willpower to stay educated, focused, and prayerful, I was able to become an entrepreneur. I am AWESOME. The fact that I had the confidence to open my own business, despite all I had been through that could have left me hopeless and useless, is just amazing. In fact, it really confirms how blessed I am to know the power within.

When I first embarked on my salon, I was excited about the financial wealth I could create. The future looked great, the sky was the limit. But something completely unexpected happened. Working with clients in the intimate and private setting of a treatment room, the women receiving attention and care in a relaxed environment, opened up deep and personal conversations. The stories of pain I heard smacked me right in the face. Not only did this make me face my own pain, I realized that so many women are disempowered and stuck in a place of hurt, where they numb themselves and push away not just their tears, but even their feeling sad. Accustomed to forget or gloss over, unable to forgive and find peace.

While I cut and styled customers' hair, I heard life stories of illness, of grief from military widowhood, economic hardship, addiction, and domestic abuse. I saw my clients' inner beauty and strength emerge as I helped them look more beautiful, listened with empathy, and offered advice. Their improved self-esteem helped them to change their lives.

As I saw my clients become empowered, I healed in the process as well. I realized what I had to offer. My resilience and firsthand knowledge of the power of forgiveness clicked with my discovery of this powerful channel of sharing my gift of beauty in every shape, form and fashion. I decided to close my salon and fully commit myself to making a lasting difference in the lives of women and girls. In 2010, I started the nonprofit organization *Empowering Through Beauty*, whose mission is to empower women and girls to live a vibrant future by restoring hope, dignity, and confidence in themselves and their communities.

With the help of my *Empowering Through Beauty* team, I help people find the confidence and courage to better their lives. We have helped women secure jobs by providing a makeover before their interview. We have witnessed the power of healing through beauty with women who are recovering from drug addiction. Their faces light up when they experience the beauty products and services. Also, we create a supportive network of women who empower communities through seminars and workshops. Since its inception, *Empowering Through Beauty* has served in numerous shelters throughout Connecticut and hosted special events in Connecticut and North Carolina. Many of the women we have worked with have graduated, married, obtained housing and are living a productive life.

Just at the right time in 2012, I was introduced to OASIS, which was truly an oasis for me. The whole atmosphere and context of self-acceptance and relaxation, and the techniques I learned, offered me the perspective and framework I had been looking for all along. I loved the simplicity and directness of the techniques. I entered the OASIS Training and became an Authorized OASIS Facilitator.

Taking advantage of this great opportunity allowed me to put all of my education in psychology into practice. It changed how I work with my clients. OASIS became the basis from which I developed my own techniques to guide my clients to peace, tranquility, and endless love for self and others. I coach my clients to wellness and wholeness. I teach others to use the techniques to create self-awareness, meaning, and purpose. To this day, our OASIS Community is very important to me. Professionally, it helps me raise my skills and techniques to a higher level, and for me personally, it remains a haven where I am reminded of my purpose and of what matters to me most.

One thing I know for sure, I am wonderfully and fearfully made. An important part of my purpose is to remind other women they are blessed with the same gift.

❖❖❖

In this moment I will share my oasis with you as you embark on your journey of a meaningful life.

In your adversities, toss out "I settle for whatever" and bring in "I am victorious."

When you are put down, toss out "I am worthless" and bring in "I am a warrior and I am worth every good thing this world has to offer."

When you feel there is no one to love you, toss out "I will never find love" and bring in "I receive love from every breath I take."

When you feel you can't make it, toss out "I'll never get through this" and bring in "I am a conqueror."

When you feel controlled, toss out "I have no power" and bring in "I have all power in my hands."

When you become angry, toss out "I am angry" and bring in "Anger has no place here."

Close your eyes and see the bright blue sky with the words *Love, Joy, Peace,* and *Happiness.* Feel it with your lips, see it with your mind, and touch it with your heart. Each time you feel overwhelmed with fear, imagine your life full of love, peace, joy, and happiness. In reality you will have it if you just embrace it.

Each day pick something meaningful you can touch and feel. Choose to explore all of its qualities. This will allow you to break free of the stress you feel in your workplace or home.

Friends, I Tanisha Akinloye have so many reasons to forgive, and I realize my life is a journey full of experiences that are worth writing and reading about. With that said, I embrace my today, my tomorrow, and my forever. My hope is you will do the same.

SUSAN SEIDMAN is a Master Certified Coach who trains life and business coaches globally, and works with individuals and organizations to inspire their authentic expression through higher-purpose living.

Energy = Spirit, a simple yet empowering message that Susan, a traditional Reiki master for 24 years, embodies in her public speaking engagements, coaching sessions and coach training classes. She believes and models that in order to potentiate who we are, we need to know our true nature, one that begs to be expressed through the energy of love, compassion and service. Susan is equipped with the talents of storytelling, humor and the ability to create a deep connection with individuals and audiences alike.

e-mail: Susan@c4w.co (co, not com)
website: www.coachingforwellness.com

connections

soul sister

THE FIRST TIME I ACTUALLY MET MILLIE was over the phone, and it was a very special experience. With no distractions from the physical world at hand, we both easily flowed into a deep soul connection. We laughed as we discovered how some important life themes connected us in an unusual, yet palpable way. To begin with, we both had a really deep and early life connection with the Latin world, even though neither of us is Hispanic. Millie and I are both "Elder Women," and I say this in the truest sense of respect to our many years of life experience that have informed our level of wisdom. We knew the importance of having found a soul sister, one who had chosen an untraditional type of path early on in life. What also captured our attention was that both our adventures had catapulted us into the Hispanic culture.

As a young woman, Millie had been a missionary nun in Peru, where she had a chance to learn some Spanish. This experience also led her to know herself on a much deeper level and allowed her the strength to leave, when she knew it was time. I had left New York to live in Puerto Rico when I was 25. Not an expected move at all, considering that I am Jewish. Still, it was true to my path, and offered numerous important life lessons and insights into myself. Equally important, it also brought me into contact with people who became important members of my spiritual family. So much so that my mother

95

often teased me that she referred to me as her daughter the *Jewyorrican*. I left the Island twenty years later with many gifts, one of them my fluency in Spanish.

So there we were on the phone. Separated by distance, unable to see each other's face, but clearly connected in some other dimension where our souls shared an enormous simultaneous smile. There was no coincidence about our meeting, just a synchronized re-encounter of old soul sisters. By the end of this rather magical call, I happily agreed to sign on for the OASIS Training. And then we paused for a moment, to breathe in this connection we both had felt, enjoying a sense of a playful profoundness, knowing that this was just the beginning of something bigger.

coaching

STUDYING OASIS WITH MILLIE was uplifting and grounding at the same time. Few trainings can boast the ability to achieve both the energy part of motivation and inspiration as well as offer the practical part of practice and use. OASIS gave me both. As a partner in a coach training school, I had always recommended breathing to my students as a quick tool for centering. Now I was able to offer them more and more powerful techniques. This made me very happy, because when I can truly see potential for my own growth as well as directly share it with my students for their growth, all is right in my world!

My personal OASIS favorite is the Emergency 3-B-C. We all need to have a way to face a challenge and deflate its impending negative hold as soon as possible, especially as a coach. The Emergency 3-B-C is the answer. As coaches, we intend our inner witness to be always present, even if we know it is not realistic to believe we can achieve this 24/7. The intention itself, however, creates a connection to conscious and unconscious awareness, allowing us to register when our body is signaling a negative emotional state. As I explain to my students, no emotion is bad. What we mean by negative emotions is that they deplete our energy, instead of fueling it to take positive constructive action. Repressing the negative emotion is not a healthy option; becoming aware of it without judgment releases the depleting energy, shifting us back to a balanced state. As soon as I become aware I am confronting something that feels overwhelming or scary or stressful, I now know to breathe it out first. It might be a judgment, a fear-based belief, or just a gremlin coming by to seduce me into self-doubt. Whatever it is, as soon as I become aware of it, the power of that first out-breath is instantly activated and immediately releases the energy hold that is building and about to disturb my capacity to be centered and present.

As we discover more about the nature of the brain's neuro-plasticity, it becomes clearer how vitally important these breathing techniques are. Simply put, every time we become aware of limiting thoughts, feelings or beliefs, and breathe them out, we are releasing their stronghold on our emotions and the disempowering patterns we follow. At the same time, we are creating a new pathway to maintaining an optimal emotional balance and the capacity to remain present. With the Emergency 3-B-C we can literally release the old and bring in the new, as we also inhale that which we consciously want: peace, calm, awareness, love.

The art of coaching is based on the powerful connection that nonjudgmental listening provides. Nevertheless, we all know that none of us is so enlightened that we never fall into judgment or lose our presence by a thought or image from past experiences. Therein lies the profound importance of the Emergency 3-B-C. With awareness, all we need to do is breathe out the judgment and we are once again liberated from our ego and headspace. As we breathe in, we are freed from identification as the listener and become one with listening, allowing the magical alchemy of the coaching process to perform its transformational powers.

Whether in the shower, in a session, in traffic, in a discussion, or hearing some very devastating news about a family member who suffered a brain aneurysm—as I recently did—just knowing that we can choose to transform any moment into a vibration of love, awareness, centeredness and peace is a priceless gift to cherish.

oasis—¡en español!

MILLIE AND I WERE BOTH EAGER to bring OASIS to the Spanish-speaking world. The first step was getting the OASIS book translated into Spanish, no easy task. We accomplished this through the help of many people. Dr. Caroline Cooke, a Panamanian who had also done OASIS via TeleTraining, was the chief translator. And to make sure that the translation would successfully "cross boundaries," Latinos in other countries—México, Peru, Venezuela, and my own island of Puerto Rico—lent their wise eyes to help. We were delighted when *oasis en la adversidad: estrategias de 60 segundos para alcanzar el equilíbrio en un mundo agitado* appeared in 2009. A gold medallion on the front cover featured the words of Cesar Chavez: *¡Sí se puede!* We wanted everyone to know that they could achieve their own oasis, even in the midst of an agitated life. We were shouting, "Yes, we can!"

In a natural and organic way that seemed to be aligned to a divine plan, Millie invited me to become the first trainer other than herself to conduct OASIS Trainings. She encouraged me to bring OASIS to as many places as I could. I received and embraced this privilege wholeheartedly and with gratitude. The arrangement was a definite win-win: it gave me more important work I could share with the Hispanic community and it also allowed Millie to reignite and expand her deep desire to connect with this community.

For some reason, my mission in life has been to be a pioneer of innovation, especially in my adopted land of Puerto Rico. I was the resident Reiki Master of the Island in the '90s. As Puerto Rico became a second home to me, and my network of coaching students grew, it seemed only natural to pursue the possibility of bringing OASIS to my beloved island. Having planted the coaching profession there, I wanted my students to have this empowering option, especially since the environment there was growing more stressful.

My first OASIS offering was initiated by the president of the San Juan chapter of the International Coach Federation. I could not have wished for a more joyous and loving experience. There was a flow and connection that moved through the room with each exercise we practiced. My students shared that they noted how these simple techniques were bringing more order and coherency to their personal lives, and how they were integrating certain aspects into their work with women's empowerment groups, in their coaching, and in stressful office environments. We all shared the experience of how much difference a focused breath could make.

Since my network of Hispanic connections has now crossed over to Colombia, Ecuador, México, Perú and Spain, I look forward to bringing the power of OASIS to as many Latin countries as I can. I am sustained by my strong belief that world peace is a process of individuals creating consciousness—one breath at a time.

To you, Millie, we all say *¡Muchas gracias!*

SUSAN TOMS, RN, MS, MA, has spent the last three decades exploring ways to improve the quality of life and well-being for both herself and her clients, through many holistic modalities related to stress reduction. She brings her compassion and caring as a nurse to her presentations to connect with her audience in an experiential way.

With a Master's degree in both Nursing and Integrative Health and Healing, along with certifications in Integrative Health Coaching and Holistic Stress Management, Sue draws from a deep pool of knowledge and wisdom on many topics. She is an Authorized OASIS Facilitator and has facilitated a Perinatal Bereavement Support Group for over twenty years.

e-mail: susantoms@live.com

finding an oasis in the NICU

> I cannot and should not be cured of my stress,
> but merely taught to enjoy it.
>
> Hans Selye

I HAVE BEEN A NURSE for the better part of four decades in a large metropolitan hospital in New York City. I have worked in many areas in several different roles. The area I have always been the most passionate about is Maternal-Child Health: newborns and their families. Childbirth continues to be a miracle to me. I have spent the last fourteen years working in a Level 4 Neonatal Intensive Care Unit (NICU). My awe has only deepened as I have helped many premature babies finish their pregnancies outside of the womb with the help of technology, the knowledge of the medical team, and the loving care of the families and nurses.

The NICU is a place that few people can imagine, unless they have experienced it firsthand. Parents are trying to bond with their vulnerable infants (often born months ahead of time) in the face of uncertain outcomes, while at the same time grieving for their dream of a normal pregnancy, childbirth and homecoming. It is the perfect setup for the emotions of stress: fear, anger and depression.

The healthcare team faces challenges of its own. They are responsible for keeping up with the rapidly changing technology, the newest care options and the long-term effects of interventions, in an environment where the infant's status can change at a moment's notice. They must maintain the constant alert status needed to pick up and evaluate the subtle messages received from these nonverbal, unpredictable patients. The burden weighs heavily, especially when things are not going well or when sudden serious changes take place in the babies under their care. As adults, we feel protective. As health-care providers, we feel responsible, and we grieve our small silent losses every day.

In a place so fraught with layers of stress affecting everyone involved, support is essential: for the compromised babies, their families and their NICU caregivers. When I found OASIS in the Overwhelm, or rather, when it found me, I realized its enormous potential as a support resource.

I was introduced to Millie Grenough and the OASIS Strategies as a student in the pioneer class of an Integrative Health Coaching postgraduate certification program. Unbeknownst to the class, OASIS was integrated into our program for use as coaching techniques. Millie and four amazing members of her OASIS Community not only taught us the strategies and the science behind them—they created a safe space in which we could freely experiment with these tools. It was a unique union of coach training, core competencies, peer coaching and stress-management techniques. We became comfortable using the strategies in a coaching setting, as well as in our own lives. We discovered our ability to tap into our creative imagination to make the strategies our own, and expand them in many ways.

The techniques are not new. In fact, some have been around for thousands of years. Millie has found a way to repackage them in a way that they can be incorporated into our fast-paced, "super-stressed" culture, to allow our bodies, mind, spirit and emotions a stress break and opportunity to rebalance. What I love about these strategies is that they are easy, versatile and adaptable to one's personal situation and preference. After all, stress is a very personal experience, based on our specific triggers and our unique perception and response to them. The triggers are neutral by themselves; our minds conjure up the rest.

In our hospital, we are planning to make the OASIS Strategies part of a new comprehensive support-program model that is proposed for the NICU. The support team currently consists of a psychologist, who herself had a preemie in the NICU, the social workers and volunteers involved with the Caregiver Support Center, the NICU social workers, the NICU Medical Director, the Administrative Nurse Manager, and myself. As a Certified Holistic Stress Management Instructor, Bereavement Facilitator and Authorized OASIS Facilitator, I play an integral part in this program. I have developed several workshops for families, which include teaching the OASIS Strategies to deal with the stress of having a newborn, both for use in the hospital and later at home—this fits in with the New York State mandate for "Shaken Baby Prevention."

For the staff, the emphasis is on how the techniques can reduce the effects of ongoing stress by periodically refocusing, cleansing the mind, letting go of issues and "changing the channel" when appropriate—a reminder that stress is all in the perception of the event. Once the nurses know the strategies, they will be able to teach and reinforce their use by the families. The preemies in turn will benefit from the calmer awareness of all their caregivers, thereby reducing their stress—and babies definitely have stress as measured by their cortisol levels. It creates a win-win-win situation all around.

As a nurse, I find satisfaction in teaching and empowering parents and staff. Nothing feels better than to see the veil of despair and helplessness lift, allowing a ray of possibility to shine in. Avenues for disseminating the OASIS techniques include workshops, the weekly Parent Support Group, an OASIS Strategies video loop to be shown in the Family Waiting Room and individualized instruction by a nurse at the baby's crib-side.

The need for support is not limited to NICU patients and their families—being ill in the hospital or having family members hospitalized is universally stressful. Once evaluated through research on family and staff satisfaction, the NICU program for stress management can be expanded into a comprehensive hospital-wide initiative. This would then include any high-stress area in the hospital setting as well as office and clinic waiting rooms. The video loop can be customized with instructions specific to many different specialties and diagnostic areas. OASIS can make a difference not only in the hospital experience; it can be a useful tool carried over into all aspects of one's life.

Each of the OASIS Strategies has its own strengths and uses in the context of our work in the NICU. I will give a few of the many possible applications.

The 4-D strategy uses movement to "get out of your head," broaden your perspective and change your energy. In the 4-D

Dump & Embrace version, you name your stressors and symbolically replace them with something positive. I see the 4-D being used by anxious, angry or frustrated parents at the Parents' Support Group, or when siblings are acting up. Exploration and naming of these strong feelings can be done prior to the exercise, or spontaneously. The siblings can do it too! In allowing the children to express themselves, however silly they want to be with it, the 4-D helps them to defuse their fears. The staff can use this tool away from the patient areas, to express their own frustrations and fears, and discharge extra stress through motion.

The 3-Breath-Countdown, 3-B-C, is the most versatile technique. It creates space for the four P's: focus on the *Present*, a *Pause* for clarity, *Power* to choose/reset and *Possibility* for change of perspective and response. It is perfect for a parent taking care of a newborn. The Emergency 3-B-C, or what my friend Diane Frankel-Gramelis calls "Sigh Breathing," can be used when the parent finds him or herself in an overwhelming or frustrating situation, when they are dealing with the adjustment of being responsible for a helpless little infant that can only express itself by crying, or when parents feel they are no longer in control of their family or personal routines like sleeping (!) or showering.

The Preventive 3-B-C is a great tool when, for instance, the parent is getting ready to leave the house for an appointment—no easy feat with a newborn! This 3-B-C Mini-Vacation can be used to regain a sense of calm when patience grows thin after a long day of caring for a sometimes fussy baby. In the NICU, the 3-B-C can help staff restore their emotional balance after having dealt with an anxious or upset parent. The parents can use the strategy when preparing to call or enter the NICU, after upsetting news, before a family meeting, etc.

Cue-2-Do addresses stress a bit differently. "Changing the channel" is a way to not only gain more awareness of what we are feeling and how we are reacting, but also to consciously shift focus from an unwanted emotion to a wanted emotion. It takes practice, patience and compassion toward yourself to learn to do this in the midst of a stressful situation, where re-activity tends to take over rational thought. The familiar drama that plays on a channel is our own emotional baggage. If your reaction to a situation is stronger than warranted, it is not about "that situation," it is about some other incident from the past. This gives us the opportunity to dig a little deeper to make the connection and break the pattern. Old habits die hard. But if we persist, we are creating a new pattern of behavior and a new neural pathway.

I have successfully used a personal version of the Cue-2-Do for many years. Whenever I got behind at work, because of a really sick baby or a late admission, I would feel myself get very anxious and overwhelmed with a feeling of tightness in my solar plexus and an easily distracted mind. I would keep focusing on not being able to get everything done on time. The emotion was fear: I was on the "panic" channel. When I recognized this state, I would ask myself if it really mattered to get out of work exactly on time. The answer was usually no, at which point I would say, "Then I have plenty of time," and switched to the "everything-is-going-to-get-done" channel. Once I calmed down, eight times out of ten I would get out on time anyway, because I was able to focus again. After a while, those incidents happened less and less, as I just learned to stay on the "everything-is-going-to-get-done" channel more and more.

The 1 Stone strategy allows you to be calm in the midst of chaos and can be used anywhere, anytime. If you don't have time for ten breaths, do five or three. This technique anchors you in the present moment. It is appealing to many different populations and groups. You can pick it up quickly and can use it frequently. And its effects are noticed immediately. Your eyes remain open to stay focused on the "here and now," and not try to avoid or escape reality through imagery. You can use a stone or any object of comfort that fits easily in your hand and can be carried with you. I use a pocket angel with a crystal face, a heart embossed on her chest and the word *LOVE* etched on her skirt. It reminds me to always "come from my heart" and to practice "self-love." I have been using the strategy when I am being hard on myself and lose my ability to focus.

The beauty of the OASIS Strategies is that they can be applied in any kind of stressful situation. You can combine, expand, and modify them to your own needs. With a little imagination and creativity, the possibilities are endless. Millie's versions are the launching point, the instruments. We, in the O Community, create the music.

VIRGINIA (GINNY) KRAVITZ is the founder of *In the Current*®. As an Executive Coach and Career and Life Strategist, Ginny guides her clients to move through change with greater clarity and confidence. Known for her energy and exuberance, Ginny has a penchant for motivating others to think creatively and apply their talents for greater fulfillment and impact. Her unique approach incorporates the Five Stages of Living in the Current.

A Professional Certified Coach (PCC) credentialed by the International Coach Federation, Ginny is one of the original Facilitators for OASIS in the Overwhelm and is co-author of *OASIS in the Overwhelm 28-Day Guide: Rewire Your Brain from Chaos to Calm.*

e-mail: ginny@inthecurrent.com
website:www.inthecurrent.com

signs of hope

IN 2006, MILLIE INVITED ME to be in her first group of OASIS Facilitators. It was an easy yes to accept that invitation, because the subject of "Breaking Through Overwhelm" is one that I had been studying for years and had incorporated as a coaching specialty. Millie's research integrates the latest brain science and this provides an important context for the OASIS Strategies.

A year later, when Millie asked me to co-author *OASIS in the Overwhelm 28 Day Guide: Rewire Your Brain from Chaos to Calm*, it was an opportunity to go deeper into the practice. Millie, Jill Berquist—my good friend and fellow OASIS Facilitator—and I put our heads together and gathered ideas to help people integrate the OASIS Strategies into real life on a moment-to-moment basis. As we shared our favorite tips and stories with each other, we realized that even as we were writing the guide, we were continuing to benefit personally from OASIS in new ways.

Since then, I've used the OASIS Strategies with many coaching clients, including executives and other accomplished professionals. I have also shared them with friends and family members. Both face-to-face and long distance, I've witnessed people from diverse backgrounds, ages and life experiences benefit greatly from the OASIS practices.

One of the most powerful and inspiring examples of what it means to "Create Your Own OASIS" occurred while working with my client Vanessa, who lives in Haiti. We had just finished developing a coaching plan that outlined Vanessa's personal and professional goals, when an unforeseen event changed everything.

Vanessa

picking up the pieces

OUR WORK TOGETHER was abruptly interrupted by the earthquake that struck Vanessa's country on January 12, 2010. Knowing someone who lives in Haiti made the news headlines all the more real. I was relieved and grateful when I received her email letting me know she was okay. After taking a few months to regroup, Vanessa was ready to resume coaching. On our first call, she explained that her neighborhood in Port-au-Prince had been spared, her home was intact, and the office where she worked was still operational.

Vanessa told me that she didn't like the feeling of no longer trusting herself or trusting life. She felt powerless and extremely stressed. We decided that the first priority was to make a plan to address her stress level. She was already implementing a program for her physical health, and was also taking advantage of the crisis counseling that was available.

Vanessa recognized that intellectually she knew there was hope, yet emotionally she didn't feel it. I asked her a spontaneous question, "What are the signs of hope?" We acknowledged our own connection as one sign that she was not alone. Did she see any other signs? "Yes," Vanessa said, "people's resilience." She saw resilience in the faces of people who had lost so much and were still going on. At the end of our conversation, Vanessa made "noticing signs of hope" part of her coaching assignment. She also decided to start the *OASIS in the Overwhelm 28 Day* program. "Overwhelmed" certainly fit how she was feeling, and the idea of following a daily guide was appealing to her. The recommendations and assignments seemed doable and just the right amount to focus on each day. While there was so much around her that was out of her control, this was something tangible that she could take action on.

one week later

THE NEXT TIME WE SPOKE, Vanessa reported two more signs of hope. "The first is that I've been able to move out of a low vibration. The second is that a friend made me laugh... That I can still laugh is a sign of hope." What a wonderful sign indeed. We laughed together for much of that call, even as we worked. Then she told me about her experiences with the *28 Day Guide*. Now, on Day 7, she was amazed at the impact of such simple changes. She noticed that the first OASIS Strategy, the 4-D, was helping her to be more aware of her environment and more connected with her body. When I taught her the second strategy, the 3-B-C, she said, "I felt my heart open." Signs of hope come in many forms.

week by week

BY DAY 17 in the *OASIS 28 Day Guide*, Vanessa reported that she was looking at things differently and without drama. By practicing Cue-2-Do she was more aware of when she was "making a story," and could be more objective now. By the fourth week, Vanessa was getting creative with the OASIS Strategies, and for the 1 Stone meditation she chose to hold her cherished rosary beads in her hands, in place of a single river stone.

Utilizing the *OASIS Guide* and applying other insights from coaching, Vanessa concluded, "I don't have to carry all those things. I can shut it down and empty my mind." It also became clear to Vanessa that it was time to do something different, something that involved fun, creativity, and expressing herself. We set out to explore those possibilities together and that, most definitely, was a sign of hope.

Some months later as our coaching concluded, Vanessa announced her resignation at work and was focusing in on her next career move. Regardless of the specific job, she was certain it was time to take a step toward, as she expressed it, "what I'm here to do… to make a difference in this country."

where do you see hope?

THOUGH THE SCALE CAN VARY GREATLY, as humans we all experience devastation of some kind over the course of our lives. I recently spoke to a woman who was at Ground Zero in New York on 9/11. Flying on an airplane triggers her PTSD, and so it is something she avoids. Yet when her elderly aunt was in need, she booked a flight to Florida and, tranquilizers in hand, got herself on a plane. I told her how awesome it is that her love is apparently bigger than her fear. She said that getting on the plane is a sign of hope for her, because it means her life is now expanded to include the possibility of air travel and vacations to new places with her husband.

What periods of devastation have you come through in your life? Is there any rubble you are sorting through now? Look for signs of hope in the eyes of others and be the sign of hope for those around you.

PETER HIMMEL is a retired physician who has practiced Internal Medicine, Rheumatology and Physiatry. He was the owner and medical director of the Himmel Health Center, a multidisciplinary clinic specializing in arthritic issues as well as fibromyalgia and the chronic fatigue syndrome. He previously was Assistant Professor of Community Health at the Brown University School of Medicine.

Peter's vast experience in the medical field enhances his current work as a life coach. He frequently partners with his wife Nancy, a licensed Marriage and Family Therapist; they work with individuals and couples as well as give talks and workshops.

e-mail: himmelhealth@gmail.com

the stress spectrum and oasis strategies

IN MY MORE THAN THREE DECADES OF MEDICAL PRACTICE I have been a passionate and avid student of psychology and psychiatry. My practice and studies, more recently enriched with my experience as a life coach, have led me to a perspective regarding the neurological basis of stress and the effects and consequences of being exposed to stressors, from minor to long-term traumatic stress.

As many studies demonstrate, techniques such as deep breathing, meditation, visualization and creating awareness of bodily sensations can have a great impact on stress-related conditions. Millie Grenough's *OASIS in the Overwhelm: 60-second strategies for balance in a busy world* offers us such strategies in a highly accessible, quick format. My intention in this essay is twofold: 1) to talk about the biological and neurological aspects of stress, and the role of these processes in serious and often ill-understood health conditions, many of which involve chronic deregulation of the nervous system; and 2) to give examples of how use of the OASIS Strategies may improve the symptoms of these conditions.

the physiology of stress—the stress spectrum

I VIEW STRESS AS AN IMBALANCE in how our body functions that requires a rebalance to maintain health. This imbalance can manifest along a whole spectrum of intensity and "realms," starting out as a physical phenomenon, manifesting in the chemistry and biology of our bodies, and eventually in the cognitive, emotional and behavioral realms, as thoughts, emotions and behaviors.

In looking at stress on a spectrum, let's first consider a very simple, mild form of imbalance: a cool raindrop falling on your hand, causing a noticeable but small irritant. Such a sensation or minor stressor is "dealt with" solely by our autonomic or unconscious nervous system, the ANS. This system has two parts that balance each other and maintain balance in our body. One part, the *sympathetic* nervous system, activates/excites specific structures in our body by releasing the chemical noradrenaline at the nerve endings. This excitation is then rebalanced by the *parasympathetic* part of the ANS, which secretes a chemical called acetylcholine through the *vagus* nerve, bringing the system back into a state of calm. In the example of the raindrop: the sensation of the raindrop activates the sympathetic nervous system, which then activates deep structures within the brain, among others both amygdalae. We then take an action, to either ignore or act upon this stimulus, and possibly wipe the drop off our hand. This in turn engages the parasympathetic system and calms the excitement in the nervous system, which in this case was minimal, and returns us to balance.

Thus the ANS works like a wave, as on an oscilloscope moving up and down until it reaches a balance point. In this example, the sensation of the raindrop on the skin of the hand has little intensity, so the excitation (the upward curve of the wave) is small, and the following calming response, the parasympathetic response (the downward curve), is small as well.

Now let's turn to a more intense stimulus. Say we get

caught in a rain shower. In addition to the sympathetic nervous system activity described above, in such an event the adrenal gland, which sits on top of our kidneys, would be engaged to produce the hormones cortisol and adrenaline. This releases enough energy for the body to be able to run under an awning for protection; more sugar and oxygen becomes available in the bloodstream for use in the brain and all muscles, allowing the heart to pump faster, and causing increased breathing and readiness for action. Here the parasympathetic system needs to react more to rebalance the system, as the upward curve of the sine wave is greater with the greater excitation.

In a simplified view, the stimulus-response chain described above has a "tipping point." Limited stimuli are handled by the sympathetic nervous system and rebalanced by the parasympathetic system, which is on automatic pilot. But in the case of extreme stimulation, the sympathetic nervous system can reach a state of being temporarily overloaded. Mammals have evolved so that if a stressor is too great, they switch from a state of great excitement to paralysis. In this state the parasympathetic nervous system takes charge for a period of time. This is considered a successful evolutionary strategy for survival. Freezing, or playing dead, can cause a creature to go unnoticed—until there is an opportunity "to escape from becoming lunch," as stated by R. Sapolsky in *Why Zebras Don't Get Ulcers* (1993). To stay alive, animals go into a parasympathetic state (shut down) and stand still, fall to the floor, or faint. After the danger is over, most animals quickly go back to a state of balance.

In humans, a parasympathetic state can be brought about

by experiencing helplessness, lack of control, marked danger, or fear of death.

complex traumatic experiences

IF A PERSON IS EXPOSED to many smaller stress-evoking events or traumas in his or her life, especially as a child, the individuals experience a continuous or even chronic "roller coaster" between the extremes of high sympathetic and parasympathetic states. This can lead to either a permanently underactive sympathetic nervous system, which shows as a state of numbness or being withdrawn or even dissociated, or, on the other hand, a hyperactive sympathetic nervous system, which manifests as hypervigilance—watching out for danger all the time.

During my years of medical practice, among other roles functioning as a psychiatrist at a general hospital and most recently during my experience as a life coach, I have found that stress affects virtually all systems of the body. As a practitioner, I have discovered a remarkably high occurrence of childhood or adult trauma in patients with fibromyalgia, chronic fatigue syndrome, headaches, irritable bowel syndrome and myofascial pain (lower back and neck).

Many of these ailments are not recognized as biologically based, nor therefore as "real" medical conditions, but rather are seen as imaginary, psychosomatic. However, these conditions are what Dr. Robert Scaer, author of *The Body Bears the Burden*, labels as "neurosomatic," in that the long-term deregulation of the ANS is a prominent source of these symptoms.

Treatment of these neurosomatic conditions should most

definitely include stress-reducing strategies that activate the parasympathetic nervous system, and thus balance the engrained stress response.

balancing our systems

THE *OASIS* 60-SECOND STRATEGIES are just the right medicine: they offer stress-reducing, balancing strategies in a highly accessible, quick format. The OASIS book gives clear information regarding the neuroscientific basis of stress, as well as the brain's ability to recover and relearn, which is known as neuroplasticity. The strategies work at many different levels. I will discuss two in more detail below.

Millie embeds her four strategies in stories. A story appears to have a primal or archetypical place in communication between humans. It evokes emotion and has personal or societal meaning. It acts as an anchor for the strategy presented.

In the 1 Stone strategy, when we're invited to focus our complete attention upon the object in our hand, we are encouraged to stay in the present moment, the "Now," as Eckhart Tolle calls it in *The Power of NOW*. Here we in fact meditate. As the eminent mythologist Joseph Campbell wrote in *The Power of Myth*, any time we are totally focused and attentive, we are meditating. Campbell gives the example of a bank teller who's counting money. This type of focused activity activates the ridge-like structures of the outer part of the brain, the cortex, and in particular the prefrontal lobe. The enhanced activity in this area "slows down" the activity in the amygdala, which is the primitive center of fear. Thus simply holding the stone and giving it complete attention can activate the more developed, "human" part of the brain, the prefrontal cortex, and reduce the stimulation of the fear center. This in itself decreases the stress response.

There is an ever increasing amount of literature about how meditation reduces the experiece of stress, leading to increased emotional regulation, internal awareness, clarity, and sensitivity with interpersonal relations, thus reducing the overall experience of stress.

The OASIS Strategy Cue-2-Do invites us to become aware of a *bodily sensation*—in the belly, the low back or neck, a temperature change in the hands, a tic, clenching of the teeth or fists—and then of the *associated emotion*—fear, anger, sadness, etc. To make the strategy practical, we call these associated feelings *emotional channels*, as channels on a TV or radio. As with the 1 Stone, the act of shifting the focus from reactive fear to conscious awareness of one's environment, for instance by watching a flower, can immediately reduce the stress level. It also gives the practitioner an enhanced sense of personal control over his or her reactions to situations.

For most people, the Cue-2-Do strategy is not always easy or readily available. It builds on a certain body awareness to identify the physical "cue," whereas many in today's society live more in their heads than in their bodies! This strategy intentionally focuses on encouraging all of us to build a clearer awareness of our bodies.

One prominent thought about the origin of emotions is that they actually stem from bodily sensations. It is a fact that our intestines have as many nerves as our spinal cord. Many of the nerve fibers that travel from the intestines to and from the brain are from the *vagus* nerve, the parasympathetic nervous system. Ninety percent of the fibers carry messages from the bowel to the brain, whereas only ten percent bring messages from the brain to the bowel. We might say that the bowel talks nine times more to the brain than the brain does to the bowel. Who hasn't had a "gut sense" or said of a stressor that they "felt it in their gut" first?

Frequently, sensations in the present moment are based on unresolved trauma from earlier childhood. An observation, sound, smell, thought or sensation may trigger a person to experience the newer cue, emotion or thought as associated with "danger," when in reality it is based upon old trauma. As such it may bring up old emotions, thoughts and possibly actions that are not appropriate for the present situation. Daniel Goleman, in *Emotional Intelligence* (1995), calls this type of brain response "emotional hijacking." Cue-2-Do helps us to undo or loosen this stronghold by "changing the channel."

Whether it's the gut, the neck, or any other part of our body, it seems clear that these pains are cues to let us know that something is going on that needs our attention. I had the pleasure of working with John Sarno, MD at the New York University Rehabilitation Center. As explained in *Mind Over Back Pain* (1984), Sarno asserts that a lot of back pain, lower neck pain, and headaches are related directly to stressful emotions. His message is simple: if we change our response to a stressor, our back pain may diminish or cease. This is done by developing a story around the stressor that the individual has the power to modify. However, addressing the pain directly with movement or massage is also necessary. Brain and body have to be addressed together.

As I stated in the beginning of my essay, my intention was to talk about stress and its impact on serious and often ill-understood health conditions, and second, to suggest how use of the OASIS Strategies may improve these conditions. To give a complete description of these intentions would take up more space than is available in the context of this book. My hope is that I have given you information that is useful to you, and maybe I have even inspired you to read more on the subject.

I strongly believe that the simple OASIS Strategies offer us a low-key and accessible approach to deal with our modern-day stress, as well as a possible first step in dealing with reactivated trauma by "grounding." The strategies have a sound foundation in modern science and research, and they are eminently suited to the demands of our overly busy lives. My hope is that this discussion has enhanced your awareness as well your desire to actually integrate one or more of the OASIS Strategies into your daily life.

To our health!

DINA MARKIND is a personal life coach who guides people to have more joy, and move from burnout to well-being. She is a certified coach through Coaches Training Institute and the International Coach Federation. Her coaching business, *Heart of Well-Being*, focuses on working with health care professionals, to revitalize their lives.

Dina: "Though I did research for my MS in nursing on the relaxation response on blood pressure, I spent years thinking I didn't need *that*. Life caught up with me and I needed to make some changes. Some of my experiences came together when I became an Authorized OASIS Facilitator. The OASIS Strategies are integrated into my coaching."

e-mail: dina@heartofwellbeing.com
website: www.heartofwellbeing.com

take a breath and refresh

WE ALL FACE MANY CHALLENGES in our lives, as well as difficulties, when we experience stress. At these times we don't always think clearly or behave the way we would like, let alone in ways that serve us and others. OASIS in the Overwhelm Strategies provide the pause that grounds me. They allow me to reconnect with what is important and then act in a way that is more beneficial to myself and to others. I like to say that they provide a pause with a purpose.

I come to OASIS as a life coach and nurse. The effectiveness of relaxation techniques to decrease the stress/fight-or-flight response is well documented and researched. My Master's thesis in nursing, written over 25 years ago, was about the effect of the relaxation response on blood pressure. Over the years, I have used relaxation techniques with many people. Working on the cardiac floor in the hospital, there were opportunities to teach patients simple breathing techniques and their benefits in decreasing blood pressure and improving health. While working as a home care and hospice nurse, I would often encounter overwhelm in the patients or the caregivers. Here again I was able to teach simple focused breathing techniques.

OASIS techniques provide the pause with added benefits. Each of the strategies involves paying attention to breathing. Breathing is so important and basic that we use it as a vital sign to determine health status. Breathing with a focus to pause allows us to settle down and return to a calmer state. When you were young, weren't you taught to count to ten prior to responding when frustrated or angry?

What is particularly special about the OASIS techniques is their clarity and simplicity, and that each can be done in sixty seconds or less. They are organized in descending order from 4-D down to 1 Stone, so they are easy to remember, and they have an element of fun. They don't require a lot of time, as for instance a body scan or guided imagery exercise would. The techniques are easily accessible to everyone, and can be done anywhere. No equipment needed, just readiness on the part of the practitioner.

Using OASIS not only helps in the moment; it has a ripple effect and allows the practitioner to lead a calmer, more aware and joyful life. This internal effect expands to others as well.

Since the strategies are explained elsewhere in this book, I will highlight some of the ways I like to use OASIS, personally and with clients.

The 4-D technique is particularly helpful for the young or restless. It is also a great deal of fun to use with a group, to loosen people up and shift energy. So often we say things like "It's all in my head." When it comes to anxiety, anger, sadness and other experiences of stress, guess what—it's not all in the mind—it's in our bodies, too. The 4-D allows us to engage our bodies, shift our mind's focus, and refresh with a few deep breaths. The four stretches in the four directions get our blood flowing, our muscles moving, and our minds shifting. There is always a sense of pleasure after doing a 4-D. Sometimes people are a little self-conscious at first, but loosening the body helps release the smiles that were held back by tense jaws.

A variation, 4-D Dump followed by the 4-D Embrace of what we want to take in, is a fun way to create positive energy for oneself or a group. Recently, with a group of Visiting Nurses we dumped paperwork, interrupting phone calls, difficult families and time pressure. With the psychic space now available we embraced joy, cooperation, calm and grace.

The 3-Breath-Countdown is the technique that comes most naturally to me, and I use it often, mainly for prevention. A variation of the Preventive 3-B-C is an Intentional 3-B-C. As an alternative to or in addition to looking at something concrete to draw positive energy from, I put a gentle focus on concepts like collaboration, inspiration, harmony. I breathe these in and bring them with me, setting the tone for my day or specific next activity. The intentional focus helps me bring these qualities into being. I like to do it before getting out of the car to prepare myself for what comes next. Prior to using OASIS, I used to sigh a lot without being aware; now I take control by breathing with intention, to be calmer even before the start of an activity.

Although the Cue-2-Do strategy requires a little more awareness, what my clients and I get back is worth the effort. Approaching bodily sensations with curiosity and distinguishing between what is really going on right now and "internal drama" allows for perspective. Asking ourselves what we *can* do about a situation and if we *want* to do that boils the situation down to a manageable level and then offers us choice. With choice we don't feel so powerless, and that already starts to reduce our stress level. Engaging our physical body helps us engage our focus. The examples below demonstrate how this works.

One of my clients reported feeling "inadequacy" and "fear" in his abdomen when he thought about work, even on the weekends. When asked what he could do to avoid these feelings, he responded, "Work," but he did not want to work while visiting family and he decided he would change the channel. When asked what he wanted to replace the fear with, he identified "confidence." We started exploring. Initially, this was odd for him, since he kept thinking this was all only about mental attitude. But once he stood up and tested a few areas of his body, he found that his confidence resides in his chest. We practiced bringing confidence in, by drawing his hands to his chest as he said the word "confidence" to himself. His reaction: "That feels much better."

It was amazing how simple the action was, once we found it. What a great experience it was for both of us, to see the relief that he expressed in words as well as on his face, and the more relaxed body posture that came along with it. Using the activity of bringing in the confidence to his chest gave him a physical act to reinforce the idea. He created muscle memory to go along with the concept. Neuroscientists say this kind of reinforcing reflects that "cells that fire together wire together." Over time, by practicing his gesture with intention, my client was able to shift more quickly from inadequacy and fear to confidence.

A woman I worked with felt her stress in her shoulders. Upon looking at it more closely, she discovered feeling guilt for not being able to meet the needs of everyone around her. She wanted to replace this feeling with self-compassion and self-acceptance. This client is a hairdresser; interestingly, the motion she came up with to bring her desired feelings in was circling the crown of her head as if drawing a magical halo.

The 1 Stone strategy also encourages us to use our bodies, by engaging our senses of touch and sight in noticing the stone's weight, color, shape and design. Many people I work with like the neutrality of the stone, the natural connection to the earth a stone has, its enduring quality, the idea that on some level the universe is made of "stone stuff." After people try 1 Stone, they will often say things like "Whoa, that was relaxing," or "That was powerful." Teaching in groups, I have found that the energy in the room shifts by the end of the ten slow easy breaths. A hush comes over the room and people are less restless. Some people feel self-conscious with the length of breathing, as did I initially. I was used to working with my breath in yoga, but mostly in sets of five; taking ten slow breaths seemed quite long at first.

My favorite experience teaching 1 Stone happened when I taught it to a 13-year-old boy while I was working as a camp nurse. The boy had a history of health issues, and was getting anxious that they would return at camp. I picked up a couple of stones from outside the infirmary, and brought the boy in where we could practice. We did 1 Stone together, and I could see the anxiety melt from his face and his whole body become more relaxed. He liked the technique a lot. Now he, too, could carry his calm in his pocket!

You can use a stone from nature, or a different object. It is helpful to use something small so you can hold it in your hand, and that is easily available, like a shell, or even a coin. I use my mom's engagement ring, which I received from her when she was dying. The stone is a diamond which is made of carbon, one of the key elements of life; but even more important for me, the ring is associated with the foundation of love that I come from. I can just rotate my ring so that the stone is on the palm side of my hand, look at it, take my ten breaths, and ground myself. From here, I am more ready to face my present situation.

The 1 Stone is so simple, yet really can be powerful. I encourage you to find an object that will work best for you. Try it out. Look around your home; perhaps there is something that draws you to pick it up. When you're out, look down and around; is there a stone that attracts your eye? Pick it up and use it.

OASIS is simple and flexible. Experiment with all of these strategies and see how you can make them your own. If you're looking for a guide or support to integrate the strategy into your life, all of us are available to you.

Be well.

Almost 20 years after receiving a Master's degree in Child Development, **ELANA PONET** earned an MSW in 1990. Over the years, Elana and her husband, Jim, have worked with hundreds of students at Yale University, where Jim has been the Jewish Chaplain for the past 33 years. Elana is the Director of the Hillel Children's School at Yale, an informal, creative Hebrew/Sunday School at which all of the teachers are Yale undergraduates. Her work more and more involves listening to and counseling undergraduates as they discover what is most important in their lives.

Elana has lived in New Haven since 1981. Before that, she and Jim spent eight years in Israel, where three of their four children were born. She is enjoying being a grandmother immensely!

e-mail: elana.ponet@yale.edu

a peaceful oasis moment in israel

AS FIGHTING CONTINUES IN THE MIDDLE EAST, I am comforted as I recall the calm that an OASIS exercise inspired during the summer of 2007.

My husband, Jim Ponet, the Rabbi and Yale Jewish Chaplain at the Slifka Center for many years, had taken groups to Israel several years in a row. The summer of 2007 was our first time doing this together.

The trip was intended to give a thoughtful view of both ancient and modern Israel. In our group were about 17 Yale undergrads, one or two who had just finished freshman year and a smattering of juniors and seniors, and a couple of graduates. We were met in Israel by a group of six or seven Israelis, most of them having recently finished their compulsory army service.

Our goal was to form a group and to expose them all to a variety of views about modern Israel, all in the context of appreciating the beauty and power of the country, its long history and its people.

Having done the OASIS Training with Millie that spring, I realized that being in the desert was the perfect setting in which I could provide a group of questing young adults with a taste of OASIS.

During the summer months the heat of the sun is too intense to do much moving around, so we were enjoying some time in the shade sometime between 11 AM and 2 PM, after finishing a hike with a knowledgeable guide.

There was something about the magic of the desert that moved me, and I led our group through 1 Stone, the OASIS technique that was inspired by Thich Nhat Hanh.

As a longtime reader and admirer of Thich Nhat Hanh's teachings, I felt particularly drawn to this OASIS Strategy. It occurred to me that since Thich Nhat Hanh had spent years dealing with the suffering and conflicts of Vietnam, engendered by years of civil and foreign wars, his methods might enable our group to confront the heartbreaking ongoing struggles between Israeli Jews and Palestinians. So much of the discourse about Israel ends up in a heated discussion about the rights and wrongs of how Israel handles the ongoing conflict with the Palestinian population that lives in their midst. The summer heat mirrored the intense heat of the situation, *Hamatzav*, the Hebrew idiom that refers to this ongoing condition.

On the other hand, summer is also vacation time, especially for students. The group was just getting to know one another; the budding connections were buzzing in the arid August air.

So I offered them a technique that Millie had taught us in our Pioneer OASIS Training.

"Find a stone, a twig, something to hold during this process," I invited them each to do. In the sandy Negev this is not very hard.

Our cadre of 19- to 25-year-olds had come with open hearts and minds for this summer experience. I can hardly imagine a more engaged group to test my newly-learned technique with.

What a way to focus their energies!

New smells, new vistas—for many of them a first-time visit to the country and a new language and way of life were being encountered.

There we were, sitting near the heart of where Jewish history is said to have begun. It is a place that works as a magnet for imaginations that have been fed by the images of Jews wandering in the desert on the way to the Land of Canaan. Biblical stories seem to come alive in this part of the country.

We sat on the ground together, took deep breaths and clung to our talismans. We smelled, observed, rotated them in our palms, ready for their powers to penetrate.

And that is when the real magic of the OASIS Strategy took over.

There was a shared joyful experience as a response to the 1 Stone exercise. Before, in spite of everyone's openness, the group was still guarded, with expectations, insecurities and unavoidable resistances in play. The 1 Stone time-out proved to be a wonderful tool to bridge our differences and unite us.

This is how I explain what happened. Concentrating on holding and getting to know the stone in hand, each in his or her own way, allows for a calm focusing and ease, a way to relax the ever-busy mind. As one does this, the whole body has a chance to slow down, and magically, hearts open at the same time.

When we first meet new people, we tend to guard our own separateness and sometimes perceive others' uniqueness as threatening. This seems quite natural. Holding and becoming familiar with something as small as a stone possibly helped deflect some of these anxieties. A stone picked up from the ground went from being an object to being more like a supportive friend.

1 Stone helped us along in the process of becoming a united group, a bond that kept growing in the course of our travels. The group loved the 1 Stone strategy.

I can guess that at least some of us continue to carry a stone in our pocket—maybe the one found that day in the Negev desert. Hopefully a memory lingers that leads us back to the quiet sense of connection each of us felt on that day. It can be tapped into anytime, anywhere.

This is an example to me of how OASIS can help still the mind. Through simply holding a stone, overwhelming emotions may find a place to land and settle. A new group that comes together necessarily experiences self-doubts and expectations, feelings that cloud perceptions. Learning how to release those feelings can be difficult. It may sound strange, but a quiet moment with a stone can be a very effective way of coming into our own center of energy and calm. From that place, one is able to be *Present* to what is really happening. Sweet irony, that a stone serves to soften our inner fears and self-doubts, which releases the openhearted dimension of us all.

In a place where stones are often thrown in anger and frustration, how lovely to imagine everyone doing the OASIS 1 Stone technique...

VIRGINIA ANN GRIFFITHS believes that everyone has the inner strength and ability to bring balance to their lives. Most people just need help figuring out what this looks and feels like for them. Believing that God never gives us more than we can handle, Virginia uses her expertise to help her clients organize, prioritize, and execute the tasks, events and responsibilities that are a part of their daily lives, so they can find the calm amid the commotion of life.

Virginia considers her coaching a collaborative effort, whether it's working one-on-one, leading seminars or workshops, or speaking from the stage.

e-mail: weleapcoaching@gmail.com
website: www.we-leap.com

finding the calm

I WAS INTRODUCED TO OASIS IN THE OVERWHELM in 2013 at an International Coach Federation chapter meeting where Millie spoke about her upcoming training for facilitators. Many of the coaches present spoke very highly of OASIS, and I felt myself drawn to it. So much so that I tackled some considerable hurdles in my schedule and signed up for the training. Woohoo!

Getting to the training at the Mercy Center in Madison, CT, was another hurdle. Hitting traffic jam after traffic jam, I arrived a few minutes late despite leaving extra early, and I felt stressed out and guilty. But Millie welcomed me into a peaceful and relaxed atmosphere. Where I had planned to rush home at seven, I found myself changing plans and staying through dinner.

The training was illuminating. I experienced what it is to be truly peaceful, focused, curious and present. While playing with the OASIS Strategies I made deep connections with my fellow attendees, people I had never met before. I learned how to listen to my own body, what emotion I was feeling and where I was feeling it. The most important piece I took away that day was that no matter what negative feeling I experience in the moment, I have the power to change that feeling to a more positive one. All it takes is to be aware of my negative state, and choose a strategy to help me shift my negative thought to a more positive thought.

I vividly remember my first real-life experience using an OASIS technique. This was another travel situation, where I had left early for a networking event to allow time to collect my thoughts beforehand. The traffic was horrendous and I was beginning to feel overwhelmed by the stress of being late, feeling out of control and trapped, with no other choice but to inch forward in this senseless parade. As I was yelling at the traffic, hitting my steering wheel, and about to call my husband to complain, I had an epiphany: use one of my OASIS Strategies. Duh! I chose the 3-B-C. I drew in my first breath, let it out, pulled in a second breath and released.

On my third breath I was still not really feeling any relief, so I remembered to look around for something to focus on other than the traffic. I decided the safest thing was the car emblem ahead of me. I drew in another breath, held it for a moment and then blew it out along with the negative feelings I had about the jam I was in. Then I inhaled a cleansing breath with a positive thought and again held it for a moment before releasing. After two more breaths, I came back to a calmer me. It was refreshing to change the channel of my negative emotions. The 3-B-C is a perfect strategy while driving: you always have access to your breath, a focal point and your thoughts to change your emotional channel!

In my practice as a Parent Time Management coach, I work with families in different configurations—one or both parents, with or without children present—on stress management and planning and scheduling. Being a mother of four children myself, I am intimately familiar with the challenges modern parents face. They are overextended, stressed, and feel that there's just not enough time for them. And that's true for both moms and dads. These are stressors I myself face.

However, each day, as I continued to use the 60-second stress-management strategies, I noticed that I was inviting more peace into all aspects of my life: with my family, myself, and my business. I was able to approach my life with more clarity. My family received the attention they needed when they needed it; being with them became pleasant, fun and quality time. When I set out to work on my business, I was better able to focus on the task at hand because my family was content! The final piece was that with family and business doing well, I was able to take care of myself. I could make it a priority to meditate and exercise, and not feel rushed and falling short. All in all, each area of my life got a more present and happy me.

My newfound clarity created a much-needed boost in my business. Before I did the OASIS Training, my coaching practice was not developing the way I had envisioned. Being present and focused opened up a couple of doors for me that I had not seen before because my mind was too cluttered. I created coaching programs for parents/families around structure and planning, designed brochures for networking and promotional purposes, and started actively pursuing speaking engagements. All this generated new opportunities.

My introductory program on stress management spans approximately five weeks and is structured around the client's needs and desired outcomes. The program makes extensive use of the OASIS Strategies. Each client has a different set of circumstances and lifestyle, so we adjust the strategies accordingly. Let me share some examples.

I worked with a family with two children. The son was easily distracted and very forgetful. The parents had tried a variety of consequences and punishments; many worked for a short period of time, but eventually the boy would forget about his responsibilities again. The parents were stuck in a cycle of getting frustrated, scolding their son and then feeling bad about that. We discussed techniques they could introduce to their son in order to help him stay focused. But I also introduced the parents to the Cue-2-Do strategy, to sort out their frustrations before reacting to the situation at hand. I helped them understand the benefits of assessing the situation before reacting to what was bothering them, to pause and think, and avoid the tears and stress.

A while after we concluded our coaching, I received an e-mail from them, thanking me. They said the Cue-2-Do provides them with the pause to realize that "most situations do not warrant the emotional investment we tend to give them in the initial moment of stress." The strategy has made a powerful difference for this family, and helped them create a more peaceful environment.

One of my clients is a single mother of four who had to make a decision on an upcoming surgery that could have potentially dire consequences. She struggled with the decision and all the statistics. At an earlier session I had introduced the 4-D-Dump to help her cope with her toddler's temper tantrums, which she reported helped quite a bit. She chose to give the strategy a try with her surgery decision, throwing away the negative predictions of death, procedure failure, fear, and lack of control of outcome, and inviting in the positive elements of faith, procedure success, her being there for her children, and love. The process of dumping and embracing helped her make a choice that she had been grappling with for months.

Not all of the work I do is centered around parents or families. Another of my clients is a banker who works in a stressful position with lots of customer contact. She used to leave work feeling emotionally drained from the negative interactions with customers. This client uses the 3-Breath-Countdown to handle stressful situations. When she sees a customer coming that she knows is upset and is going to express that to her, she uses the Preventive 3-B-C and takes a few cleansing breaths to calm the anticipation of the encounter. When she doesn't have time to reach for the Preventive, she uses the Emergency 3-B-C to release the negative feelings by blowing out what breath she has in her, along with letting go of the thought of the irate customer, and then breathing in three cleansing breaths. After learning how to use the 3-B-C and the Emergency 3-B-C, she now has options for dealing with the stress in the moment rather than taking it home with her.

A client couple that participated in the program let me know that one of their major stressors was mismanagement of their time, which caused them to bicker. They found themselves being couch potatoes after they got home from work each evening, and then when the weekend came they were inundated with household chores and errands, leaving them no quality time to relax. Their strategy of choice is the Personal Palm Pilot (Mini-Vacation). Now, instead of plopping themselves down on the couch when they come home from work, they take a few moments to take a mini-vacation, a much-needed break from the workday. This helps keep them off the couch, reenergizes them, and motivates them to do something during the week that they would otherwise have to do on the weekend.

Life can be hectic. It is a real challenge to keep all the balls in the air—and keep yourself sane, healthy, and happy at the same time. I know that all too well, with a husband and four lively children, a business I am dedicated to and passionate about, and a community to which I am devoted.

As much as I encourage my clients, I too made a commitment to remember to make room for my own OASIS! I invite you to take a Mini-Vacation with me right now.

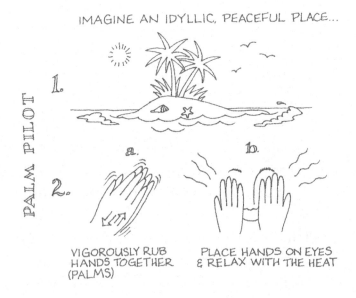

IMAGINE AN IDYLLIC, PEACEFUL PLACE...

PALM PILOT

1.

2.

a.

b.

VIGOROUSLY RUB HANDS TOGETHER (PALMS)

PLACE HANDS ON EYES & RELAX WITH THE HEAT

KAREN GOMEZ is an intuitive coach and teacher of holistic studies. She is the founder of *We Are The ONES Wellness & Coaching*, focusing her work on stress management. She is committed to inspiring individuals to trust their inner voice to help gain clarity, to be passionate and courageous leaders, and to serve others through coaching and teaching to live a fulfilling and peaceful life.

Karen is a certified Higher Ground Leadership® Coach, Holistic Life and Wellness Coach, a Facilitator for OASIS in the Overwhelm, and master teacher of yoga, meditation, and Reiki. Her unique approach helps her bring her teachings "from the yoga room to the boardroom." She resides by the shoreline in Madison, CT.

e-mail: we-are-the-ones@comcast.net
website: www.we-are-the-ones.com

1 Stone for clarity

WE ALL EXPERIENCE FORGETFULNESS and mental fogginess from time to time. But with people living longer, more families are experiencing the onset of what is called dementia with their aging parents. These types of dis-eases of the mind become stressors not only in the life of the person who is experiencing the ailment, but in the life of those who care for them as well. This is where my story begins.

My mother is now 90 years old. She was officially diagnosed with dementia in the summer of 2013, after my father had died that spring. My family knew that Mom was forgetful, but didn't realize how much Dad had kept from us. After Dad's funeral, we noticed Mom's cognitive abilities were declining rapidly. She was having trouble remembering where the cereal box was located even though it was in the same spot for 43 years, remembering how to pay the bills, or even if she had taken a shower that day.

Her confusion grew greater along with her frustration. I noticed that she didn't recall names or visits from family members, and she began to call me multiple times a day with the same questions. Being the baby of the family, I wasn't used to taking care of Mom. She had always taken care of me. I found this to be very concerning and frustrating at the same time. She wasn't my mother any longer. I needed to understand this thing called "dementia."

I learned that dementia is an overall term that describes a wide range of symptoms. These are associated with a decline in memory or cognitive skills severe enough to impair one's ability to perform everyday activities, and cause one to become frustrated, angry and confused. This was exactly what was happening to my mother. She had all of the symptoms.

In December 2013, my older sister and I finally decided to move our mother into Assisted Living. Mom was angry and confused by the whole transition. She kept asking me, "When can I go home?" Each time I tried to explain logically that it was a terrific place for her and she would like it eventually, it made her more upset and confused. She focused only on the negatives of the situation instead of on how she would benefit from being cared for in a living arrangement that would protect her. Her stress was elevating daily.

At this time, I was studying *OASIS in the Overwhelm: 60-second strategies for balance in a busy world* to enhance my work as a Holistic Life and Wellness Coach and to become an Authorized OASIS Facilitator of the program with Millie Grenough. My work focuses on stress management, using the modalities of yoga, mindful meditation, and Reiki energy healing, so it made sense to include the OASIS tools in my toolkit.

Whenever I had an opening in my busy schedule, I would go visit my mother. She was often confused and angry, and would ask me the same questions. People with dementia do this a lot. Their short-term memory is disrupted. They fixate on a certain thought and do not release it, because they do not remember the answer you just gave them, or even if they have asked the question. Many times I would leave frustrated and disappointed. I did not know how to help my mother, or how to make her happy.

One lovely spring day in April 2014, I took my mother out to lunch. As happened so often, she kept asking me over and over where she lived. I found it frustrating and was feeling sad that there was nothing I could do to help her. Or was there? On an impulse, I took out the stone I carried in my handbag since our OASIS Training; I used it to practice when I had a break in my day or to introduce the technique to my clients. I asked my mother to hold the stone. I then instructed her to take a breath and to gaze at it. I started asking her questions about the stone: "What is it? ... How does it feel? ... Is it cool or warm to the touch? ... Does it have grooves, or is it smooth?" I then asked her to breathe some more while she gazed at the rock. She did this willingly.

AMAZING! The exercise distracted her away from her repetitive questions. It rinsed her mind of her looping thoughts, allowing space for calm and peace. She then began to laugh and we started another conversation. It was remarkable how the 1 Stone strategy brought some sunshine to a lunch that would have been otherwise a challenging and rather dark situation. Instead of leaving in tears, Mom and I had a few moments of clarity and laughter that day. Who knew?

My dream has been to take what I do "from the yoga room to the boardroom." I did not expect to bring it into assisted living facilities, and especially not to my mother. She is an elderly woman who has not been exposed to many of the ideas behind my coaching programs, nor has she experienced my work. Her memory of the last 30 years has been erased, and she now doesn't know what I do, even if I explain it to her each time I see her. But why not try? One doesn't need to understand the theory behind the tools for them to work. Mom didn't need to know why or how. She came to a place of "just be" by doing.

The OASIS Strategies result in immediate relief of stress by enhancing mood, creating space for breath, and redirecting the mind to a place of stillness.

1 Stone will not cure dementia. But it can help redirect the troubling confusion to those experiencing the symptoms of this debilitating disease, and bring relief to the caretakers as well. My mother continues to get stuck in loops, getting anxious in asking the same questions repetitively. But sometimes we find our way out with the help of 1 Stone.

Thank you, Millie, for sharing your work.

For more information go to www.alz.org/what-is-dementia.asp

MARJORIE POLYCARPE is a registered nurse of 23 years with a Master's degree of Science in Nursing. She currently holds the position of Assistant Director of Nurses in Clinical Care Management at a New York City hospital.

Marjorie is also a yoga instructor. She strongly believes that optimal health can only be achieved through incorporating natural modalities in everyday lifestyles. She envisions the day she can bring yoga to the hospital setting as an alternative approach.

e-mail: mapolyca@aol.com

yoga in the overwhelm

PEOPLE FROM ALL WALKS OF LIFE and layers of society are experiencing increased stress in today's world. Working as a registered nurse, I have encountered and cared for many such people. From the stay-at-home mom, juggling to keep up with the extracurricular activities of her three children, to the Wall Street stockbroker watching over his clients' assets, to the medical professional caring for patients in an overbooked schedule, the teacher managing a classroom with 30 children with wildly differing needs, the mail clerk with ever-growing zones, the bus driver whose contract just ended, the college professor, the congressman, to the movie director, and YES, even the clergy! ALL of us are experiencing and suffering from the same problem of increased stress. This too often results in anxiety and depression.

The World Health Organization, drawing on research conducted by Medco Health Solution, reports that the number of Americans on medications used to treat psychological and behavioral disorders has substantially increased since 2001. Anxiety disorders are the most common psychiatric illnesses affecting children and adults in America. An estimated 40 million Americans suffer from anxiety disorder (www.who.int/medicinedocs).

It is now widely accepted, both in conventional and nonconventional fields of medicine, that disorders such as these should not and cannot be treated by medication alone. Psychotherapy, support groups, exercise, faith communities, personal health coaching, and modalities such as dance, music and yoga therapy are often useful as complementary approaches, and some would argue that they are useful as the first resort.

The OASIS Strategies make use of the key elements that are also in the ancient art of yoga: stillness, breathing and movement. The techniques form a natural combination with yoga practices, and can help cope with everyday stressors, thus reducing the resulting anxiety and depression. When we become "unstuck," we are able to move forward and work towards our goals.

stillness

STILLNESS IS ALWAYS THE FIRST POSE of any yoga practice, and similarly it is the first step to any of our OASIS techniques. Getting your mind and your body into stillness affords you an "edge." It awakens your awareness to YOU and your present state. Stillness can occur in seated or standing position.

When you feel anxious, overwhelmed, uncomfortable or simply "stuck," imagine yourself on your yoga mat. Your mat is your personal oasis, your safe space.

Imagine it to be your favorite color, a color that evokes calm, safety, protection for you. For some it will be an earthy tone; for others it may be bright orange or green. Whatever color it is, get on your imaginary yoga mat and come into stillness.

Allow yourself a minute to let your inner "chatter" calm down, and begin to focus more intently on your breath.

breathing

B.K.S IYENGAR, THE CREATOR OF IYENGAR YOGA, explains in his book *Light on Life: The Yoga Journey to Wholeness, Inner Peace, and Ultimate Freedom* (2005), that we bring calmness and quietness to our minds and our emotions with the retention of breath after an exhalation. As Iyengar explains, when we empty the brain of thoughts with our breath, we also empty the toxins of memory. With every exhalation and retention, we can let go of resentment, anger, envy and rancor. In Iyengar's words, "Exhalation is a sacred act of surrender, of self-abandonment." Breathing is a method of changing our state of being. It is a way of letting go of toxic thoughts in the mind and feelings in the body; hence these deep breathing exercises are sometimes called the cleansing breaths.

In OASIS we use the 3-Breath-Countdown or 3-B-C technique to perform the cleansing breath and change our negative state of being. Watching the flow of the breath also teaches stability of consciousness, which leads to concentration. The Yogic breathing techniques, also known as Pranayama techniques, are meditative in their origin and in their effect. As Iyengar states, "Pranayama is the beginning of withdrawal from the external engagement of the mind and senses, which brings peacefulness." Pranayama basically consists of four parts: exhalation, retention of the breath after exhalation, inhalation, retention after inhalation.

When we begin our deep breathing with an exhalation, we can release our toxic thoughts, feelings and emotions. Allow the exhalation breath to come out slowly through your lips, while your abdomen gently contracts.

Let your inhalation be long, subtle, deep, rhythmic, and even. This allows energizing ingredients of the atmosphere to enter in to the cells of our lungs and rejuvenate us. Invite the inhalation breath to come in slowly through your nostrils, while your abdomen gently expands. Retain the inhalation for a brief moment: this allows the energy to be fully absorbed and distributed to your entire system through the circulation of blood. Your slow exhalation will carry out toxins that you have accumulated.

This breathing technique can be practiced when you come into stillness on your mat and/or at the onset and completion of every pose. It is a simple and pure detoxification method for the whole body and mind.

Once in stillness, draw your attention to your breath... Let your lips be soft... Purse them open a tiny bit to let the air come out... Very gradually, let all the breath out... Your worries, and any emotion you want to let go of can exit with your exhale... Hear your breath going out...

Repeat this pattern three times, until you have reached the 3-B-C. If you wish, you may choose to repeat three more times, uttering the sound "OHMMM..." with each exhalation. The reverberation of your breath slowly bouncing against your voice box, as you utter "OHMMM..." brings a sense of release and relaxation.

movement

MICHAEL TAYLOR, CO-FOUNDER OF STRALA YOGA, has coined the catchy phrase, "Let movement be your medicine." He explains in his lectures, "If you want to feel good, move in a way that makes you happy. Start there and the rest of your life will follow."

The body is an intelligent machine, always sensing and re-acting to its environment. The body knows, before the mind, when discomfort occurs. When you feel discomfort or become ill at ease, your body's distress signals ignite to bring your awareness to change. Often this change can be brought about by movement of your whole body, or parts of your body. A discomfort in the mind, be it an anxious state, or a depressed state of mind, may improve with motion.

The father of modern German dance, Rudolf Laban, be-lieved that movement was generated from the self, rather than from the music. Laban claimed that movement is what creates the space around us, and wanted to liberate movement from any feeling of constraint to find total harmony of soul and spirit. (Dorr & Lantz, 2003, chronicle 26.1)

It has been stated in the medical community, over and over again, that the absence of movement leads to death. Even if the outward appearance of stillness in the body is demonstrated, we know the body internally is kinetic, always moving, with movements found in the circulatory, lymphatic, gastric, neuro-logical and respiratory systems. Outward movement of the body, which entails moving the limbs and the joints, promotes optimal functioning of the internal organs and systems. Move-ment of the body brings harmony with the internal and exter-nal self on a physical, mental, emotional, and spiritual level.

Isabella Pericleous, from Columbia University, explains in her 2011 thesis on movement and mental illness, that it is necessary sometimes to experience certain feelings and emotions directly through our bodies. In everyday life, the human body functions as a tool of communication. The research also shows that moving with others expands our sense of social connectedness, which is beneficial to lowering both stress and depression.

So it is imperative to MOVE, MOVE, MOVE your body, to remain healthy! Movement can be done alone, but ideally and most beneficially it's done in a group setting, such as a yoga class or an OASIS workshop.

We recognize these ideas in the OASIS Strategy of Cue-2-Do, in which we are reminded to pay attention when our body is speaking to us through a cue of discomfort. When our body is telling us to move, we should listen to it. The more we respond to our personal Cue-2-Do, the more we become attuned to our body. Allowing the mind to merge with the physical body, leads to wholeness.

The OASIS 4-D strategy is an ideal approach to movement. The stretches it entices you to do are similar to yoga movements, and they can be done in a short amount of time, at any place. The concept is to move the body in opposite directions in one sequence: north, south, east and west. These movements are inviting, invigorating, and make the body feel good. They make us happy! Yoga also has 4-D poses in almost every style of yoga (Iyengar, Bikram, Ashtanga, etc.).

Sometimes you may feel an urge to move in a certain direction during yoga practice. When this occurs, allow your body to move to the pose it wants to be in... there is no right or wrong pose... it could be the desire to do a head stand or the desire to go into a corpse pose—laying flat on your back into stillness.

Even in your daily life, whether or not you are in yoga practice, pay attention to your body. It is talking to you. Whichever movement your body leads you to do, follow it... The movement, consciously chosen by you, will be nourishing and therapeutic for you.

I encourage all of you to practice these simple yet effective stress-reducing techniques. Share them with your family, your colleagues and your community. Namaste!

SUZANNE DUDLEY-SCHON
is a life coach, mom, and closet poet. She earned her BS degree in psychology from Duke University, is an ACC credentialed coach with the ICF (International Coach Federation), and an Authorized OASIS Facilitator. Suzanne holds her second-degree training in Reiki, and is currently underway with her training in Somatic Experiencing—the work of Peter Levine.

Suzanne has an office space in the Center for Integrative Health, where she feels lucky to be part of a community of like-minded practitioners and therapists who hold a holistic approach to health, healing, and well-being. Suzanne lives a good life with her family and lots of dogs in New Hampshire.

email: suzannedudleyschon@gmail.com

oasis in the overwhelm—from my window

I FOUND OASIS IN THE OVERWHELM like a thirsty woman in the desert—on my hands and knees and blessed with some good fortune. And yet, it took me a while to decide. As if made paranoid by emotional dehydration, I circled back again and again to take a look at Millie's website, read testimonials, read bits of her book, before I was ready to sip. And then, finally, I drank. As you can imagine, from this stressed-out, painfully "thirsty" person, I felt immediate relief and gratitude. And that was just for signing up for the OASIS Training and reading the book.

When I actually participated in the training, it was one of those "Ahhh, yes!" moments—knowing I was in the right place at the right time. It sounds hokey, but it felt, and still feels, like an awareness of a divine plan in action. Millie created a space to learn and experience her work that was immediately safe and inviting. Then, as we all proceeded to learn the techniques of OASIS, the participants—"OASIS Sisters" as we now refer to ourselves—all settled into a delightful ease that is a rare oasis in the hectic world in which we live.

Each accessible, simple 60-second technique has its usefulness and specific qualities, and I have called upon each one since reading Millie's book and completing the OASIS Training. I have aided clients in my life-coaching business, I have helped my children and stepchildren, and I have shared it with health-care providers and others in the social services industry. Below

I describe case-specific uses of the OASIS Strategies and how and why, in my opinion, they work.

4-D: While coaching a group of volunteers who worked for a domestic violence shelter, I used the 4-D. It immediately worked to "lighten" the energy in a room. And not only with that slightly reserved group. What I note time and time again with this strategy is how the simple act of moving one's body, vocalizing, and being slightly "silly" relaxes people and seems to bring them out of their heads and more into the present. I would say to anyone, "Don't underestimate the power of goofy!"

3-B-C: Like watercress in the veggie world, the simple deep breathing of the 3-B-C strategy packs a stress-reducing, cell-changing, potent wallop. The three breaths physically change oxygen levels, heart rate, etc. I have used this tool with great success when my kids were in the grips of emotion and headed for a big blowup. The Emergency 3-B-C allowed them to get off the mental train they were speeding along on, settle down and make a clear-headed decision. This energy shift gave them the power of choice, so that they no longer were swept up in the throes of a feeling. Rather than merely reacting, they could decide how to act. What a gift it is to afford a person that precious pause in time.

The Preventive 3-B-C (Mini-Vacation) gets used a great deal in my life. I have taken my sibling from her self-declared feeling of overwhelm to a much-appreciated, reviving quiet moment. I personally have benefited from the use of this little mental getaway. When in the midst of a particularly challenging time or when just fraught with the Rubik's cube of logistics that my life often is, this technique has been a lifesaver. I am sure I have a lot more hair on my head because of it. These free mini-vacations can be just the balm needed. There is a self-nurturing beauty in the conjuring of a happy memory or creating an oasis with the imagination. To experience it both firsthand and as a witnessing parent, friend, or coach is an awesome thing.

Cue-2-Do: This strategy is complex, but combines many elements so deftly that a person can put them to use with ease. It reminds me of great art that appears simple, yet when closely examined can be appreciated for the complexity involved in the creation of it. In my coaching, particularly in cases when a client has a perceived "block," the Cue-2-Do is often just the tool to help them laser through the situation. Often these blocks consist of many components that have melded into a lump that the person can no longer separate and manage. As with the 3-B-C, by addressing and calming the physical and the emotional layer before having a person try to think through or analyze a situation, the prefrontal cortex is newly available to them. It's as if a shut door is being opened.

1 Stone: This is one of my personal favorites. I often use this mini-meditation as a way to get centered and present before a session, or use it anytime I feel scattered and not present.

stress is everywhere

STRESS IS NOT A UNIQUELY AMERICAN problem. It is a universal human problem.

Although I look pretty Scandinavian from my father's genes, my mother was born in the Dominican Republic. I speak Spanish and consider myself "Hispanic on the inside." On my travels to the Dominican Republic, I am reminded of the universal nature of stress. Just about every person I meet, from every sector of the population, no matter the age, status, income or job—waiter, guard, parent, or bank executive—all suffer from stress. How to handle stress is not part of the conversation there, as it is in the USA. There is no plethora of media coverage, meditation courses, or mindfulness classes.

Millie, having lived in South America, dedicates a lot of time to local Hispanic communities, and has provided a Spanish edition of her book. I have sent off copies in many, many directions on the map. I am thrilled at the prospect of OASIS doing its magic, with its quick and easy inexpensive strategies, in the Spanish-speaking community here and overseas.

To me one of the most wonderful aspects of OASIS is that everyone can do it and benefit. There is no socioeconomic discrimination. No cultural divide. These 60-second strategies act like a unifying principle—within the self and between people. Stress divides us, keeps us dashing in different directions, anxious and unable to give or receive love, or pretty much anything. I remember reading a little book years ago called *Love Is Letting Go of Fear*. And what is stress really, but an amped-up subspecies of fear? Seems pretty clear—if you let go of your stress—your fear about work, family, health, money, etc.— then you allow for love and connection to take its place. And this is the beautiful by-product of Millie Grenough's work. When all of us Authorized OASIS Facilitators get together in a reunion meeting, there is a sense of loving community. Peace, thoughtfulness, and caring... it is as if OASIS work is a unifying principle of stress-reduction and love.

When I remember to bring this simple work into my everyday life, it has powerful effects. I can, with a shift in my energy and thoughts, be a little version of what many of us strive for, to be that change that we are looking for. Gandhi said, "If we could change ourselves, the tendencies in the world would also change. As a man changes his own nature, so does the attitude of the world change towards him... We need not wait to see what others do."

It is my continuing commitment to help people using OASIS—from my little window in the world.

Thank you to Millie and every OASIS practitioner for these seemingly small and elegantly simple actions that make such a powerful difference... The need is universal.

RENEE O'CONNELL is Director of the OASIS Training Program and the office manager for all OASIS projects. As Millie's right-hand person since 2007, she is a vital link in scheduling, design and publication, and OASIS communications. She keeps the OASIS Community connected and up-to-date, strategizes media relations, and helps create and distribute Millie's "sanity e-notes" to thousands of people each month.

Renee is a mother of three, and plays an active part in her children's lives. She is Team Mother for her son Peter's football team, a huge fan of her daughter Stephanie's cheerleading team, and Brownie Troop Leader for daughter Abby and friends. OASIS helps Renee ride all these waves.

my journey

IT WAS A SUMMER MORNING when I received an email from my sister-in-law Julie asking if I was interested in a position working from my home as a Virtual Assistant for this organization called "OASIS." I had just left my full-time job of 13 years as a business manager, found out I was pregnant with my third child and was enjoying the time at home with my other two children. As I reviewed the job description, I became extremely intrigued and wanted to learn more about Millie's travels and what OASIS could bring me as a wife, mom, friend and human being.

I met Millie and her colleague Kate Smalley one afternoon in her New Haven office. I remember the meeting as if it was yesterday, sitting on the sofa, listening to what Millie had to offer me and telling her what I had to offer her. We just *clicked*— simply stated. Eight years later, and here we still are. We stand with an OASIS Community of hundreds of amazing, bright, inspiring individuals, a growing line of OASIS products, and a high demand for Millie's presence at workshops, conferences, retreats, you name it. Millie and OASIS are wanted and needed more than ever in today's stressed-out world.

growing with millie and oasis

WHEN I FIRST BEGAN WORKING WITH MILLIE, she had just come out with her second book, *OASIS in the Overwhelm: 60-second strategies for balance in a busy world.* I was part of the book launch together with several other passionate women—marketing hard to get the word out about OASIS as the new wave for stress relief. We wanted to let people know it only takes 60 seconds to manage harmful stress, change your channel and go from chaos to calm. It really is that simple!

Millie started presenting OASIS and the four strategies to corporate executives, women inmates, K-12 schools, health-care workers, coaches and others in workshops, conferences, retreats and small groups. There was an overwhelming positive response. Every day it became clearer to us how universal and urgent the need for practical accessible stress relief actually is.

what about moms and dads?

ONE DAY MILLIE AND I WERE IN MY KITCHEN brainstorming about how we could let parents know that they have an *out*— an easy, simple way to *just breathe* before reacting. An *OASIS for Parents* workshop was the perfect idea. I invited five of my girlfriends, all of us busy moms dealing with busy husbands and busy kids, and we had the first *OASIS for Busy Mothers* at my home. The discussion in my living room that night was hot! We shared our stresses and laughed when we found out how to use some of the simple strategies to help us.

3-B-C seemed to be the highlight for us moms. We discovered that when we were in a "no-win" situation with a child, the deep exhale and inhale of breath could calm our bodies, and— just like that—our brains could think more clearly before reacting. Instead of our usual kneejerk habit, we had a different route: we could actually pause, take a breath, and decide what to do next. Amazing!

Funny thing: our husbands heard about it—maybe they noticed the difference in our stress levels!—and asked for their own OASIS meeting. So, a month later, my husband Pete and the other husbands gathered, again in my living room. I wasn't allowed in, so I'm not sure what they talked about, but they did seem happier when they broke for refreshments in the kitchen after their meeting. We took a photo of the guys and sent it to our local paper. The media ate it up and featured a whole story about it the next week.

from the living room to the larger world

WHEN MILLIE PRESENTED OASIS to a group of coaches, the response was stronger than she expected. The coaches asked her point-blank: why don't you develop a training program so that we can learn this and teach it to our clients? We thought this was an excellent idea. Why not teach the OASIS Strategies to others so they could deepen their knowledge of the philosophy and techniques, and then teach them to their staff, clients, families, friends, colleagues?

This group of coaches helped us develop the Pilot Program for the first OASIS Training; they formed the heart of the Pioneer OASIS Training that launched in 2007. Since then, Millie has conducted 15 onsite OASIS Trainings and four TeleTrainings. There are now Authorized OASIS Facilitators throughout the United States, and in Panama, Puerto Rico, and New Zealand.

Since Millie has such a close connection with the Latino community, we were delighted when her OASIS book was translated into Spanish, and when Susan Seidman conducted the first training in Spanish with a group of coaches in Puerto Rico. Sue hopes to bring OASIS to other Latin American countries and to Spain.

a surprise in the training

I HAD READ MILLIE'S OASIS BOOK NUMEROUS TIMES and had assisted Millie with several OASIS Trainings before registering as a trainer myself. Wow, how different it was to actually be a participant! Learning and doing the four OASIS 60-second Strategies in-depth myself was an experience of "*Wake up world, a whole new me is about to move in!*"

The 4-D strategy got us all on our feet. We were told: "Shout whatever is stressing you out, invite in what you really enjoy." We were stretching, moving, shouting and laughing. Yes, laughing out loud at the words that came out of our mouths and that were so relieving:

> *Reaching North shouting "Laundry!"*
> *Reaching South shouting "Dishes!"*
> *Reaching East shouting "Cooking!"*
> *Reaching West shouting "Taxi!"*

We were *dumping, dumping, dumping* all the overloaded stress from our daily lives. The difference from two minutes prior to our very last dump was incredible. The feeling of burden was gone. The movement along with breathing out makes this strategy so simple, yet so effective.

I remember talking to Karen Senteio, another trainer in my group, about parenting. We talked about the situations that come up and the huge responsibilities that it puts on us. We shared story after story, laughed, and gave each other suggestions for coping. Karen and I were definitely comedians that day and even thought about leading a *Tips: Just for Parents* workshop, teaching the 3-B-C Palm Pilot (Mini-Vacation): the perfect 60-second strategy for anyone needing time away. It's free, you don't need to make travel or hotel reservations. All you need are your eyes, hands and breath.

I like to take this "time for me" every day, right before the kids come home from school. I make sure I rub my hands together until they are warm… Close my eyes… Put my warm hands over my eyes… Take a few deep breaths… Then go to my special place. Some afternoons I go to the ocean or a Caribbean island. Or I simply go to the sky and watch the birds glide in the air. When it's time to come back, I slowly uncover my eyes and return to reality with peace and calmness, ready to greet my children.

kids need an oasis, too

OASIS ISN'T JUST FOR ADULTS, it's for children as well. I have taught my kids every strategy and found that the 4-D and 3-B-C are the ones they use the most.

One day I had to take my daughter Stephanie, then age seven, to the dentist. She was in the backseat as we drove to the office. It was very quiet in the car, which was unusual for Stephanie. I turned my head to see what she was doing and noticed she was crying. I asked her what was wrong. She said, "I don't like going to the dentist, I'm scared." I told her there was nothing to be afraid of, and she needed to calm down. I looked at her and said, "Stephanie, let's do a 3-B-C. Take a deep breath in… Hold it… Now breathe out… Deep breath in again… Now breathe out." I had her repeat this five times. After she was done, I asked her how she felt. She said, "Mom, I'm not scared anymore, I feel better. I know I can do this." The strategy brought her back to a state of calm, took away her tears and put a smile on her face.

My younger daughter, Abby, has a hard time in school and seems to get frustrated with her homework. I taught her the OASIS 4-D strategy and told her that whenever she gets angry, to stretch it out. "Shout out what's making you flustered, and do it as many times as you need to to focus again." I can see Abby jump up, lift her arms up and shout "*Homework!*"; reach down on "*Math!*"; stretch to the sides, yelling "*Subtraction!*" and "*Multiplication!*" It always works.

Kids have many different stressors that adults don't. The OASIS Strategies are a great tool for them to use because they only take 60 seconds to be effective. My kids love them and have told me they have taught them to their friends. Now that's something to be proud of!

praise

I WANTED TO SHARE a few of the testimonials that have come in to let you know that the OASIS Strategies do make a difference.

Neerja Arora Bhatia writes:

I am diving into OASIS and I think it is brilliant, concise, to the point and a great step-by-step guide...

Here is what came to me as to what OASIS stands for:

O – Openness
A – Agility
S – Strategy
I – Invitation or Inspiration
S – Sanity

OASIS, a four-step dance from overwhelm to sanity...

Diane Loomis-Setts sends a note:

The skills you taught will last a lifetime!

Juan Carlos Galvez:

OASIS has become part of my everyday life. I am always thankful for your great wisdom that you offered me this summer! It has enhanced my spiritual, intellectual, physical, and emotional well-being. Last night, I took a jog by the lake and did a roaring 4-D—it was amazing. I think that the ducks, wolves, and other wild animals felt it, too.

Sue Wells:

We laughed, we cried, we boogied... We felt safe to open up to our co-workers, so we felt more like human beings and could see our co-workers as fuller human beings, too. Thank you.

As you can see, OASIS has made a lifelong impact on so many people. Living OASIS has changed my life. Take the 60 seconds to change yours.

DEBRA HEALEY is a heart-centered health-care leader, passionate about improving the patient care experience while empowering staff engagement. Debra has a proven track record for building cohesive, integrated teams that give each team member the opportunity to reach their highest potential.

As a person on a spiritual path for some time, Debra has a vibrant belief that we have everything we need inside of us to accomplish whatever we desire. Her goal is to share the OASIS Strategies and other stress-management techniques with others, so they can manage everyday chaos and increase the bliss and joy of each present moment.

e-mail: debrn96@aol.com

simply oasis

OASIS SIMPLIFIES MY OVERWHELM! I met Millie in 2007 at a healthcare conference. I noticed her immediately for her sparkling energy and colorful booth. What also caught my interest was the name of her book, *OASIS in the Overwhelm*. The name intrigued me. I am the administrator of a home health and hospice agency, and part of our patient assessment is completing a long and comprehensive form that coincidentally is named OASIS. When I met Millie at her booth, we talked about the title of her book. I commented that our home health professionals had a need for her OASIS Strategies to cope with their "OASIS" overwhelm in completing that detailed assessment! Our relationship began that day. I bought every item on Millie's table and brought the information back to my office to share with my team.

Over the next year, I read the book and absorbed all of the OASIS Strategies. I loved their simplicity so much that I decided to attend the OASIS Training to learn more. The training gave me a deeper appreciation for the stratagies' magic and brought new friendships that inspired me to dig a little deeper to share Millie's message.

My deeper "dig" led me to sponsor an *OASIS in the Overwhelm* workshop for our staff. I brought Millie in for an entire day to share her OASIS Strategies. We offered three sessions, so everyone, from all departments, would be able to attend. I expected that the licensed clinicians would welcome the opportunity to learn about another type of OASIS. But to my surprise, the support staff that signed up outnumbered the clinicians two to one! During that day, I learned that the demands of work placed as much stress on the support staff as on the clinicians who treat patients. The clerical staff members shared the stress they experienced due to the hours involved with typing, printing and sending out paperwork to physicians, and the pressures and frustration of dealing with multiple conflicting needs and demands on their time. The personal care aides expressed the stress involved in providing patient care at a very vulnerable time in the patient's life.

When we got started, staff generally thought that the OASIS Strategies we offered were just too simple to work. By the end of the day, having worked with Millie, literally everyone embraced the simplicity of the strategies as a touch of magic. Each staff member received an *OASIS to Go* pack at the end of the workshop as a thank you for attending and a quick way to remind themselves that the strategies are there to use whenever needed. Since the workshops, I have had several follow-up sessions with participants. They report they still successfully use the strategies to combat everyday overwhelm and chaos.

I've been grateful for the friendship I've formed with Millie through OASIS. We've collaborated on ideas that provide other options for the OASIS Strategies to be experienced. One of our conversations addressed the Catch-22 dilemma that so many clinicians are caught in: too busy to attend a workshop to learn to calm everyday chaos. Millie provided an answer. She developed a DVD and several YouTube videos that expressly provide a way to learn the basic strategies quickly.

I shared the video with some of the clinicians who had not attended the workshops. After overcoming initial negative associations between OASIS and our challenging patient assessment, the videos have indeed allowed a quick access to the strategies. 1 Stone seemed to strike a particular chord with many clinicians, and offer them a way to take a deep breath in the midst of "busyness and chaos" and find a moment of calm. The *OASIS to Go* pack with its stone was received as a gift of just a little simple wisdom that worked. A hospice clinician reported that she carries the stone with her; after patient visits she holds the stone to honor the exchange that has just taken place with the patient and to center herself for her next patient visit.

what oasis strategies mean to me

I'VE EMBRACED OASIS for over five years now. What I love most about the strategies is that they are simple, yet steeped in science. They are easily available to everyone; the research on neuroplasticity provides evidence that the strategies work.

I must share that it did take a while for me to incorporate each strategy into my everyday life. Though I knew and understood each one, months went by where I didn't use them. Then, one day during a very hectic time, it occurred to me: that I was tuned to a negative channel and I could do the Cue-2-Do and change that channel! I decided at that moment to take a breath and experience the negative feeling that was occurring, name it my negative channel, and immediately switch to the positive channel. Quite simply, it worked! Since that day I decided to consciously add these strategies to my "toolbox" of coping skills. They have become second nature, a way to get instant relief and coping for everyday stress challenges.

I use the OASIS Strategies in different ways, depending upon the situation. I've used the 4-D in meetings when we needed to change the energy. I've found that staff enjoys using variations of the 4-D to clear out whatever stress may be lurking or unspoken in the moment. For example, in a stressful budget meeting we used the 4-D strategy to clear out all the demands of revenue and budget cuts, to bring in new energy for renewed budget success. I've used the 3-B-C to center and focus before important meetings and presentations. Cue-2-Do provides a quick way to change the channel in the midst of a stressful situation. I've adopted some special channels—for example, changing from the "anxiety" to the "bliss" channel in an uncomfortable situation. In fact, you can change the channel, do a 3-B-C, throw in a 4-D and be in an entirely different mood in a matter of seconds!

I've developed my own morning routine that sets the tone for my day. I call it my "one-minute miracle." Though I use this routine in the morning, it can be tapped in to any time of day to gain a moment of bliss. I begin with a morning centering meditation and use the 1 Stone strategy during this morning meditation. For one minute I hold the stone and chant, pray or say out loud my intention for the day. I sit in the moment to feel my presence and still myself, just for one minute. Holding the stone helps clear out the sleep cobwebs and sets the intention for the coming hours.

OASIS Strategies serve as a reminder to love yourself, to tap in to that eternal peaceful place inside, and calm whatever chaos is coming up. Use the strategy that fits the moment, change that channel and cleanse yourself of the current moment's anxiety. You have everything you need inside of you!

Millie opens her book with a quote from Jon Kabat-Zinn, PhD, who said, "You can't stop the waves but you can learn to surf." I've learned to surf using the OASIS Strategies.

OASIS in the Overwhelm—simply brilliant!

DR. SHEILA M. KEARNEY, CPC, BCC, is a certified Strengths Executive and Well-Being Coach. She brings more than 25 years of experience as a coach, consultant and researcher.

During her tenure at the Gallup Organization, Sheila was a founding board director and executive director of the International Positive Psychology Summit, an international forum on Strengths and Positive Psychology. Previously, she served as a foundation director and program officer and as a Boston Public Schools teacher. She earned her Doctorate and Master's degrees from Harvard University in Administration, Planning and Social Policy, and a Master's degree in Educational Psychology from Boston College.

e-mail: sheilamkearney@gmail.com

adaptations in an inner-city classroom

I BEGAN MY PROFESSIONAL CAREER as a teacher with the Boston Public Schools System. I can still vividly recall my first day, walking into a class of 15 Special Education-Resource Room students. My fear and anxiety during the first week or two soon subsided and were replaced by a sense of having found my purpose in life. After graduate school and a long career in the private sector as an executive manager, I made a vow to seek opportunities to teach and inspire young, diverse and at-risk students.

Now, working as an independent Strengths Executive and Well-Being Coach and consultant, I've had the honor to teach weeklong summer courses to inner-city high school students for the past four summers. The objective of *Strategies for Success*, a privately and publicly funded program, is to teach critical skills for workplace and life success, such as timeliness, workplace attire, etiquette, positive attitude, effective and appropriate communication, respect of self and for others, accountability, and so forth. I consider it a worthy venture to help provide a foundation for these students that will help determine their current and future well-being.

As those of you who have ever taught public school students know, the abilities (cognitive, developmental, emotional) and attitudes in a classroom vary dramatically. In the urban community and school district hosting the *Strategies for Success* program, the students come from diverse backgrounds and many different language environments. Moreover, many of the students have intensely complicated lives, facing factors themselves or in their immediate environment like HIV-AIDS and other serious illnesses, mental health problems, incarceration, violence, foster care and the lack of a loving and supportive family.

Teaching such a complex classroom is a challenge, to say the least. I liken it to "trying to lead a group of 30 cats successfully across I-95." Moreover, the different curricula offered these last four years have been ill-suited for this savvy urban inner-city youth population (that is, too childish, lacking sophistication), and not appropriate to keep a busy, variously skilled group of students on point and fully engaged. This year, I took the liberty to add the OASIS Strategies to my teachings. Here's what happened.

On the first day, following their lunch break, I asked the class to stand. I announced that we were going to do a new exercise that is used in more and more workplaces to enhance the mind-body-spirit connection, the 4-D. The kids didn't care too much about why we were doing it, but creatively adapted the exercise into a dance movement—hip-hop style. What more can I say? They enjoyed the 4-D, so we used it before every class and after every break. I observed that this exercise helped students bring their focus back to the objectives of the program. It became a ritual to let other issues, clutter, etc., go so that we could get back to the objectives of the program.

As a classroom management style, teachers-in-training are often urged to set a point of attention; for example, standing quietly at the front of the class, a 5-4-3-2-1 countdown, or distraction techniques such as a bell, flicking lights on and off, and the like. This year I utilized the 3-Breath-Countdown for that purpose. Once I had class attention by a 5-4-3-2-1 countdown, we followed through with a 3-2-1 (3-B-C) countdown. I'm not a physio-psychologist who can explain the dynamics in doing this practice, but I noticed that it helped my students relax, clear their minds and get ready for instruction.

Using the OASIS 1 Stone during the first day of class, I coached a meditative/visioning exercise with students focusing on the goals of their week-long course: what they would learn, and how they would utilize this during their first workplace assignments and in their lives.

This was an exercise I found particularly useful when interacting one-on-one with a few students who either reported to class early or sought my time after class to ask advice or just talk. One particular student comes to mind: a young 18-year-old student who was mother of two children—one recently diagnosed with ADHD. As she was about to begin community college, she was interested to learn how she could best help her son, a soon to be pre-kindergarten student. Sharing about 4-D and 3-B-C, we adapted a strategy that she could teach both her children—her son in particular—to use when distracted and in distress.

Day by day, I observed my students become more comfortable with the exercises. They related to them. Most of the kids had never practiced such forms of meditation/mindfulness, as they never find time to quiet their thoughts and never-ending life noise. This was the first time they had experienced what it was like to be deeply focused—and at the point of peace. The practice offered meaningful moments, and conversations about mindfulness and how to use it when faced with life's pressures and stresses.

At the close of the last day of class, I had a real sense of accomplishment, having led my 30 "cats" through the program curriculum and certification. From what I saw, I believe my students will incorporate the strategies into their complex lives, as they are about to be adults. OASIS helped make a difference.

I am grateful to be a member of Millie's O team. I send 4-D, 3-B-C, Cue-2-Do and 1 Stone to you all with love!

SUZANNE A. ROSENBERG is a board-certified case manager and licensed clinical social worker with 25 years' experience in behavioral health, home health and hospice. During that time, she presented at community, state and national venues on hospice, palliative care, end-of-life decision making and pain management.

Suzanne is currently the director of a psychiatric nurse case management program and provides staff training on motivational interviewing, case management practice, and compassion fatigue. Suzanne is also a strong supporter of sustainable agriculture and food justice. She is one of the founding members of a community farm in Woodbridge, CT, which donates over two tons of food a year.

e-mail: srosenberglcsw@gmail.com
website: www.linkedin.com/in/suzannearosenberg

changing the channel

WHEN YOU'RE CONSTANTLY ON OVERDRIVE, it doesn't take much to push you over the edge. Being of the subspecies "workaholic," I rarely get up from my desk and leave the building during my workday. But after one particular meeting, where I was called to task in a particularly condescending manner for something that was completely out of my control, I just had to move.

I got in my car and drove out to the main road, up the hill to the next town and into a parking lot. I had a clear view of the town below me. My heart was pounding, I was dizzy and my mind was full of dangerously racing thoughts. My throat was tight and my eyes burned with unshed tears of humiliation. Then I let Millie's voice into my head—"Is there anything you CAN DO and WANT TO DO about the situation?" (I just LOVE the way she says that, so I've recorded it into my long-term memory.) I was on the "you're no good" channel. I'm a manager, and I cannot do my job on this channel. Did what I was feeling really have anything to do with what just took place? The infernal internal dialogue! Is there anything I CAN DO—yes, resign and walk out! Abandon my team! Have no income! And no, I did not actually WANT TO DO any of that.

I run a psychiatric nurse case-management program, and I love my team. No one works harder and more compassionately than they do, with such a challenging (and challenged) group of people. I'm not ready to leave them. And besides, I'm good at what I do. I was simply having a "flight" reaction to a perceived threat, a primitive response that bore little relation to the actual circumstances.

People we work for may confront us, say things that hit us where we are most vulnerable and not even realize they are doing so. Some people are adept at letting these remarks just roll, and move on with their day without missing a beat. Others internalize them, brood over them, question the speaker's motives, question their own motives. We all have our triggers, whether it's at work or play, with bosses or parents, co-workers or lovers or children. But how much of our time and energy do we want to spend processing the past, doing the internal cleanup and readjustment necessary to be present and future-oriented again?

I have wasted a lot of time on all this counterproductive rumination. I was over 30 years old before I finally learned that I could make a mistake and admit it without my world coming to an unnatural end. I decided that I needed to spend a lot less time on these torturous mind games.

I had been hardwired to have alarm bells go off in my head and body at the slightest suggestion that I'm not perfect. I used to think of it as a groove that is worn into my physical brain, like a "skip" in a vinyl record. Fortunately, I've learned some useful things about the neurochemistry of the brain. I was greatly relieved to learn that the brain is more like a computer than a record player. Unlike a record, the brain can be reprogrammed. I did many different things to reprogram that pesky organ: cognitive-behavioral therapy, journaling, Landmark Institute trainings, shamanic journeys, Fourth Way. All of these things made my dear brain very well prepared for the remarkable reprogramming shortcuts that are the four OASIS Strategies. They were delightfully familiar to me, and are utterly brilliant in their deceptive simplicity.

The OASIS Cue-2-Do has given me one of the best shortcuts ever to "change the channel" and disconnect from the unpleasant emotional impact of relatively insignificant events. The technique is powerful for a number of reasons: 1) it requires you to become present with what is happening in your body (which often knows more than your mind!) and to define what emotional state is being generated, 2) it asks you to determine whether this emotion is related to the present or the past, 3) you get to make a choice to do something about your situation, or decide that you don't need to do anything, and 4) you get to choose to experience a different emotional state, selected from your vast repertoire of previously experienced emotional states.

As I sat in the car on that lovely late summer day and decided not to quit my job, I gave myself permission to simply *be* in the clarity of the present moment, to experience myself as enough for whatever task or challenge was placed in front of me. This is my "equilibrium" channel, where my energy moves to my belly, so my throat can open and my voice can find its way out again.

The four simple OASIS Strategies, although they are the distillation of extensive amounts of theory and research, can be taught quickly and to anyone, regardless of prior experience. I decided to bring the 1 Stone strategy to my team of nurses in our weekly staff meeting. The nurses generally work from home and see each other only once a week. After spending the week on the telephone and on visits, coaching psychiatrically and medically ill people, you might rightly imagine that they are rather anxious to talk to one another. Add to that the stress of having to deal with constantly changing documentation processes, and you can easily envision that our meetings can become somewhat intense.

One meeting morning, I gave everyone a stone. I asked them to hold it, feel it, look at it, and notice its features. After some initial sounds of skepticism, the room grew quiet. I suggested that they give themselves a gift, the gift of taking ten breaths while being present with the stone they were experiencing. The room became still. The only sound was breath. The shift in energy was palpable, almost visible, as the space inside and outside our heads cleared. I saw gentle smiles curl onto relaxed faces. There was a feeling of compassion at that meeting that is not always present as we discuss the rigors of our work. It was a valuable reminder to me of the power of this work, and the change that is possible in only a moment or two.

Since I've experienced the OASIS Training, I remember to breathe with awareness more often. I remember to remind my staff to breathe, and to pick up their stones. And they remember to tell their clients to breathe, to take three deep breaths, to start with an exhale when their anxiety threatens to overwhelm them. Together we build momentum to bring more calm to our corner of this crazy world.

My life still presents me with the same challenges and triggers. But using the strategies, my reactions have changed.

When I catch myself running old tapes, I remind myself that my brain is a computer, not a record. I Cue-2-Do and change my channel. And I can do that because neuroplasticity is not just a theoretical construct, but is the very nature of our brains. You can change your brain, and your emotions will follow.

LYNNEA BRINKERHOFF,
founder of *Radical Nourishment*™,
is a board-certified Executive/
Wellness and International Coach
Federation PCC-level coach and
board member. She brings 25
years' experience in operational
and strategic roles—in hospitality,
health care and professional service—and works with leaders
in transition who seek greater results, purpose and resilience
in life and work.

Co-founder of the StressSquad™ and the first East Coast
Ecotherapy program, Lynnea is a seasoned integrative health
practitioner who continues to seek remedies for modern-day
maladies. She authored chapters in texts and journals ranging
from the neuroscience of leadership to organizational align-
ment and equine-assisted coaching.

e-mail: www.eponadevi.com
website: lynneabrink@gmail.com

it's not how many times you fall...

IF THIS CHAPTER DOES WHAT I WISH it to do for you, dear reader, it would result in these three things:

You leave this chapter saying to yourself:
"Wow, if it's really that easy and can be applied in almost any situation and bring me greater peace and ease, I am IN."

You feel:
"I am not alone. I feel affirmed, relieved, hopeful, curious, willing and empowered."

You will:
Take one strategy and apply it in less than one minute, and get your life back, moment to moment, by pressing the reset button.

first line of defense when faced with peril... breathe!

WHEN BASKETBALL PLAYERS ARE SET TO SHOOT a basket amid a myriad of extreme distractions (screaming crowds, waving banners, yelling coaches and more), they are taught to take a game-changing, critical breath, as they aim and shoot. Before they release the ball they release their breath. The same holds true for police officers who are taught to take three deep breaths before they pull the trigger on their gun. Millie Grenough's four key OASIS Strategies counsel us that breathing with intention and following a simple but not simplistic 60-second strategy, could well be the only thing needed to rebuild sanity in our streets, in our offices and our homes.

If the athlete, the officer or the regular person holds onto their breath at the moment of taking critical action, a surprising percentage of their resourcefulness goes off line. Tension is too high in the body, leaving the brain and muscles to starve and suffer almost immediately. The body cannot function properly and loses its capacity to "hold the charge" of the additional pressure it is under, and rash decisions are often made.

Simply put, our performance goes down when we hold our breath. Consider a drunk who falls on the sidewalk. They rarely get hurt! They hit the ground with utter trust and do not "worry" about how they might feel after the fall. They do not waste energy anticipating what could go wrong. They are simply in the moment and literally roll with the punches, more so than a fully cognizant person who allows their mind to rule and therefore tightens up and often holds their breath. Challenge yourself to relax completely at the moment of impact. Releasing breath at the most anti-intuitive moment could literally save your life. You become more expansive and allowing. Consider holding the charge, not the breath.

the art of the fall: relaxing with intention

I AM PASSIONATE ABOUT PRECISION SPORTS. I golf, do archery, whitewater kayak, and skeet shoot (where clay pigeons are hurled across a field randomly, as we seek to take aim and hit the target in fast motion, slowing down the action by our breath and intention alone). In all these sports, one is required to drop the energy out of the mind and trust the body's natural wisdom and its innate "homing device within." We can be sure that Tiger Woods did not think his way to stardom!

I am also a martial artist. I practice Aikido. *Aikido* literally means: "The way of unifying with life."

合 – ai – joining, unifying, combining, fit

気 – ki – spirit, energy, mood, morale

道 – dō– way, path

In Aikido, we are thrown around on the mat a lot. When I first started, I held my breath during each fall, thinking somehow this would help me stay safe and cope with the inevitable pain I would experience on impact. But this only made it worse! I was taught *ukemi* instead, "the art of falling." We are guided to "breathe on the way down," to release ourselves to the ground intentionally rather than allowing ourselves to be thrown down without a sense of balance or control.

I discovered that when I do this, I remain supple to the fall, am able to spread out the impact of the blow across my whole body, avoid injury and enjoy the ride. *It doesn't matter how many times I fall; when I use my breath well, getting up again is easy.* The tendency to hold our breath under duress or in anticipation of what's going to hurt is second nature. Letting the breath go is utterly counter-intuitive—the result however, is miraculous and restorative. We all need our practice mates (*Ukes*) to remind us of how to best take care of ourselves when we fall.

Ukemi: The art of the fall

The lesson I learned from this physical practice goes beyond the mat, and is changing my life. Breathing with attention has become my one non-negotiable guiding light and fail-safe strategy at my most critical moments.

Neuroscience would remind us that we have a gap between stimulus and response. Author Stephen Covey used to say, "The key to our happiness lies in how we use that gap." *Is this not the essence of the ubiquitously referred to concept of mindfulness?*

As a reminder to "fall well" and to trust that you will rise again, try this variation on the OASIS Preventive 3-B-C:

> Breathing in – *life comes to me*
> Still moment – *life is with me*
> Releasing out – *I go to life*
> — adapted from Deepak Chopra

the big "O"
(as we might call it in some circles)

O-ASIS... OH-ASIS... Hoooommmm-e-O-stasis...

However one cuts it, the OASIS Strategies are infectious, because they are easy, accessible, doable and give immediate results; beginning and end of story. It's as easy as 1, 2, 3, 4... and 60 seconds... really... Below are quick examples of how I grab hold of the strategies for myself. Try one now.

1 Stone: Focus with your eyes open on the details of something natural; breathe with the phenomena you see and allow yourself to take in the majesty of this creation as you turn it about in your hand.

Cue-2-Do: Notice your default tendency when something difficult arises; exercise free will as well as "free won't" and decide for yourself how you wish to think about and approach the situation in question.

3-Breath-Countdown: Whether you are in a present emergency or are anticipating something you dread, take the time to oxygenate your system by focusing outward on something pleasing and inhaling or simply exhaling with gusto and allowing air to rush back in, feeding you for your next effective step.

4-Directions: Simply reach up, down, to the right and left side of yourself to experience the pleasure of stretching the spine and your perspective at the same time. Say whatever words are most accessible to you that you either want to embrace or release. (For instance, "north, south, east, west" or "open, closed, up, down" or "sky, earth, left, right.") Keep it easy and within reach. Feel the value from the opening and the sloughing off as well as the drawing within.

For more detailed information on the OASIS Strategies, see elsewhere in this book or Millie's *OASIS in the Overwhelm: 60-second strategies for balance in a busy world.* Most importantly, use the strategies and make them your own.

holding the charge

THE OASIS STRATEGIES HELP ME in key moments when I am lost, forgetful, tight and contracted. I come from a family that did not teach us kids how to control basic impulses. Many walls had holes in them from family members punching and kicking them, due to hot tempers and violent outbursts. While I was a fairly steady kid, the only benchmark I had for expression of frustration was the way everyone else in the house expressed it.

Embarrassingly, the concept of self-regulation was not discussed as a valuable skill to have once launched into the world. When strong emotion would rise, I had no capacity to "hold the charge," nor did I see value in it... until I had made several missteps and was baffled at the residue I had left in situations over the years. I was into my twenties when I discovered the importance of maintaining my equilibrium with a mindful edge toward my impact on others, and how vital this ability is in becoming a valuable member of society. Self-regulation is now my full-time occupation, and it has created more connection and opportunities than I could have imagined.

athletes of life

SIMPLY IN THE COURSE OF OUR DAILY LIVES, we all meet athletes' challenges and dilemmas. Times are intense and turbulent. We live 24/7 lives at a high level of consistent tension, putting us on high alert and taxing our sympathetic nervous system. Author Carolyn Myss speaks about this as the only time in history that we are having deep spiritual awakenings and have to pay our taxes at the same time! (*Anatomy of the Spirit*, 1997.)

It is difficult not to get hijacked by the daily drama. As in sport, we often tense up in anticipation of pain and difficulty, forget to breathe and make our problems much bigger than they need to be. We do, however, have the power to redirect our deeply engrained knee-jerk responses to challenge and stress, and bend our arc from overwhelm toward greater health and happiness.

lessons from the mat

AIKIDO TEACHES US TO "UNIFY WITH LIFE." When an Aikido master is attacked, he or she resists temptation to meet aggression with aggression or to harm an "attacker." Instead, they seek to blend with the forces that are coming at them. From the stance of "do no harm" and with as little effort as possible on their part, they disable the destructive energies and redirect the attacker through an emergent creative solution.

What "attacks" us in everyday life is usually a highly personal, individual experience that typically catches us off guard. Our physiological responses, however, are intended to serve as guides and give us our own sense of empowered choice points. Like an Aikido master, we are required to remain in contact with our emotions as "signals of our system." We must have self-awareness, and "get off of it," let it go, release our breath when we are least inclined to and "breathe mid-throw" (yes, on the way down). This allows our vitriolic egos to fade into the background and enables us to tune in to the larger mission of what is being called for.

you too can do this...

IN ALL OUR "PERFORMANCES," be it in sports, relationships, work, or traffic, we all are presented daily with opportunities to be "in practice" and to do so with an attitude of inviting what life is offering up. This gives us a chance to unify with life, harmonizing with and not railing against what is presented, thereby raising our chances for bettering both the results and the satisfaction we so dearly seek.

Author and original positive thinking master Napoleon Hill did not know scientifically what we know today about neuroplasticity, but he knew from personal practice that we must become steadfast in adhering to an optimistic point of view, by sealing off the negative impulses to things that can bring us down. Our brain can take the high road, instead of just the same old well-worn pathway of doom. But it does take mindful practice, over a sustained period of time.

This is the promise of the OASIS Strategies. To allow us that moment of respite to "choose again," to press the reset button and face life afresh. I invite you to greater freedom, ease, power and peace through your own simple practice.

Go ahead... Take 60 seconds now... Try one...
May you be met with an unexpected ease of being...
And may your next few hours be ones of your choosing...
Ready, set, reset...
Are you in?!

 The word that best describes **KARIN JOY WHITLEY** is ENERGETIC! Her mission in life is to help inspire others to find passion, joy and energy within themselves. A 2011 ICF-CT Coach of the Year (CPCC, PCC), she specializes in leadership, productivity, onboarding and career development coaching, and is an Authorized OASIS Facilitator.

Karin Joy holds degrees in Corporate and Organizational Studies, and in Marketing and PR. In her role in HR as a Corporate Training and Development Specialist, she focuses on communication, team building and presentation skills, incorporating humor, fun and experiential learning. Karin is a regular blogger for *The Huffington Post*.

e-mail: karin@karinjoywhitley.com
website: www.karinjoywhitley.com

oasis in the corporate workplace

FOR THE PAST EIGHT YEARS, I've been assigned to spearhead the wellness initiatives of our company. We are in the energy industry, and my role is Corporate Training and Development Specialist in Human Resources.

Our company has truly committed to the physical, mental and emotional health of our employees. We have a dynamic Wellness Team of ten employees, who all understand the importance of a healthy workplace. We have created what we call a Wellness Wheel, consisting of all the components to cover when we take care of ourselves: the financial, spiritual, mental, physical, emotional and social realms. We work on the Wellness Wheel in "Lunch and Learn" workshops, and address topics like college and retirement. We've also introduced alternative healing modalities: chair massages, reflexology, educational sessions on Reiki, acupuncture and naturopathic medicine, meditation, yoga and "laughing at lunchtime." Brain exercises to improve our memories and to sharpen our cognitive abilities are incorporated into our day.

A recent reduction in our workforce had caused an enormous increase in the stress level of our employees, who had to deal with multiple priorities, deadlines and increased expectations. We received more and more requests from the employees to find ways to reduce the stress in not only their work life, but personal lives as well. It became clear that we urgently needed to find a stress reduction tool for them.

I researched stress reduction options that would be most beneficial, easy to learn and most effective. At this time, I had the good fortune of being trained in OASIS in the Overwhelm's four 60-second strategies by my newly-met colleague, Millie Grenough.

As I began to practice and learn the strategies, I found that I was trying them out at home, at my desk, in the car, and in public places. These strategies immediately reduced my stress, reenergized me and assisted me in controlling my emotions. I even felt I could refocus at work with a sharper awareness.

Now, how could I get our employees on board and share these effective strategies with them? I saw two problems. First, I knew that everybody always felt they had no time. Second, certain employees were hard to reach. They had not partici- pated in any of the other lunchtime stress-reduction programs or methods that the Wellness Team had offered in the past, usually citing scheduling conflicts, or being "too busy," or not feeling comfortable in a group setting. I had to come up with a creative way to reach and teach everyone.

The great thing about the OASIS Strategies is that they were actually created by Millie for the individual who has a full day, every day. So that took care of the first obstacle.

To tackle the second obstacle, I decided to offer the option as a one-on-one instruction in my office, anticipating that this idea could open the door to many employees, male and female, who wanted privacy and confidentiality. I purchased *OASIS to Go* packs so that our employees could take away a tangible re- minder of the strategies.

Here's the email I sent out:

To: All Employees
Subject: 8 to feel GREAT!

Are you looking for tools to help you de-stress in your daily life?

How about giving me 8 minutes of your time, one-on-one, to learn four 60-second strategies to use when you need to energize, calm the mind, change your reaction to a stressful interaction or refocus?

OASIS in the OVERWHELM Strategies by Millie Grenough

Please respond to this email so we can arrange a time for me to teach you either in-person or over the phone.

Your family, friends and co-workers will thank you AND want you to share these strategies with them!

Karin Whitley, PCC, CPCC
Corporate Training & Development Specialist

Within two days, seven employees had signed up to learn the OASIS Strategies! Two of them were men—remarkable, since usually mostly female employees registered. The first manager who requested to integrate the 1 Stone strategy was male and had two additional men on his team. Each of his team members was going through a personal crisis, and he felt that if they could all learn the same technique they could support and remind each other when they recognized their teammate was getting stressed.

Since then more employees are asking to learn the strategies every month. Managers are incorporating these stress-reduction techniques as a closing to their team-building events.

I found that the men identified with the strategy of the 1 Stone the best. Men like something tangible that they can hold on to, keep in their pocket or wallet. I have a police officer who keeps his stone in his pocket so he can readily utilize this effective stress-reduction tool. One of the men I taught the four strategies to was involved in a tragic motorcycle accident two weeks later. He was confined to his bed for three months. He now had something in his stress reduction toolbox to get him through the anxiety and trauma. I felt that I had given him the "gift of calmness."

The 60-second strategies can be shared in a time frame acceptable to everyone's busy schedules. Our lives have become more and more fast-paced and packed with so much stress. It is vital that we find ways to manage our stress and to assist others in having a healthy and happy work life.

I am thankful and proud that the managers in our company are recognizing that they need to be aware of their employees' stress level and assist in finding ways for their staff to effectively handle the increasing work demands along with their day-to-day stressors at home.

I hope more and more companies will do the same.

 **ANGELA McGRADY** worked for the US Army's Care Provider Support Program as a Resilience Coordinator, a job in which she used all of the OASIS techniques in her classes and briefings. She is a Compassion Fatigue Educator and a Traumatic Events Management Facilitator, and has provided service to many professionals suffering with secondary traumatic stress.

Angela is a US Air Force veteran, with an MBA in Healthcare Administration. She provides resilience training and has facilitated resilience workshops to help others calm their busy lives. Angela is married to Michael McGrady; they have raised three wonderful children: Kayla, Stefanie and Mike Jr. They currently reside in Colorado Springs, CO.

oasis on the front lines

WHAT IS THIS WOMAN DOING? I said to myself. I felt out of my comfort zone with this 4-D stuff. I'm a very quiet, inward person. But there I was, standing in a room full of people, raising my hands above my head yelling, "*North!*" Then bending down, stretching as far as I could go, hollering, "*South!*" Reaching as far left as I can, "*East!*" Right, "*West!*" And you know what? It felt good! I stretched my body, filled my lungs, I laughed. It didn't matter what others thought of me, the stresses of the day seemed minimal; I was in the 4-D zone.

I work as a trainer and resilience coach; I teach and facilitate resilience, burnout and compassion fatigue classes with soldiers and civilians in health-care settings, both providers and administrative staff. Many employees in a hospital give so much to their patients and clients that they forget to give back to themselves, which can cause an imbalance in their lives and even burnout. I help people find the calm in their lives and be productive and alive.

I was introduced to OASIS in a training workshop that Millie taught to the trainers/coaches in our Care Provider Support Program. I wasn't sure if these simple strategies would be a good fit for the population I work with, but much to my delight, they were! Here are some of my experiences.

shake it off!

I INTRODUCED THE 4-D OASIS STRATEGY to a small group of nurses who deal with work stress, but can't easily leave their floor and take a break. The 4-D offered them a set of skills, and a quick mental break, so that they could focus again on the task at hand: to care for their patients.

Some of our administrative employees had the same problem of not being able to leave their desk. They complained that eight to ten hours working on the computer wreaked havoc on their bodies. The physical inactivity and constant staring at the screen caused stiff muscles and joints, and left them exhausted. Getting up and moving around would be the ideal body break, but often they couldn't. For those situations, the 4-D is the perfect alternative. We practiced the 4-D both sitting and standing at our desks. The hint that we could say any word instead of *north, south, east, west* caused much laughter and offered a stress reprieve. I heard these comments afterward, usually said with smiles:

I think I'll do this often; it feels good to stretch my stiff muscles.

I probably won't do this in front of customers, but I will definitely do the 4-D on my breaks!

I'll do it with my co-workers and share it with my patients.

The 4-D is also a very good way for a team to start the day together, or come together midday for a huddle.

I've personally used what I call the 4-D-Doodle during long meetings and trainings. It's known that doodling helps relieve stress and memory function. I like to draw flowers; when a 4-D is added to the doodling, flowers are pointing in all directions! It relaxes my tension, clears my mind and emotions, and helps me stay focused.

breathe it out

CALM YOUR MIND. WHAT DOES THAT MEAN? I, like most people, always have a million things running through my mind. Did I turn off my curling iron? Are the dogs out? Will my boss like my presentation? Are the dogs in?

Why do we humans ruminate on every little thing? Worry is such a waste of time. Especially about things that are out of our control!

We seem to live in a chronic state of fight or flight, being overwhelmed by pressures at work, in our families, about money. When issues pile up, we no longer see the difference between big and small things. And when we feel overwhelmed, we lose sight of others and don't take care of our relationships, at work and at home. We become sullen, angry, or depressed, and we may just take those emotions out on others through our actions or inactions. This alone adds another stressful issue to our ever-growing pile of stressors. The negative spiral feels never-ending.

A good breathing technique helps calm the mind. The OASIS 3-B-C strategy is one of the easiest to teach and learn. When a technique is simple, it takes very little effort to put it in practice. And when someone sees nothing but stress in his or her life, easy is what is needed. But wait! How is breathing going to take away all of the stress that I'm feeling and how is it going to fix my problems? I'll describe this through some experiences of real people.

I remember the time I worked with a group of soldiers in what was for them a requisite annual resilience training. They were initially not interested in this "fluffy stuff," felt they were too busy, and could handle their stressors on their own. I introduced the OASIS 3-B-C strategy to them. They liked the name, because acronyms are how soldiers communicate. I asked them to make a list of things that moved them into a state of stress, and a list of things they enjoyed doing. Next, I asked them to focus on one of the things that caused them stress (the job, a supervisor, home, etc.). We talked about how their bodies felt when they did this. Some of the comments were: "My heart is beating faster," "My face is flushed," "I'm feeling angry or annoyed."

They were feeling the stress just by thinking about this negative list. Then I asked them to invoke the 3-B-C: inhale and exhale three times while resting their hands on their stomachs, reminding them to perform this slowly and deliberately. Next, I had them think about an item from their "like to do list," while continuing the 3-B-C. After a few minutes, all of the soldiers said that they felt better, calmer. Some reported they felt a lower heart rate. Every one of them said they would use this in an actual stressful situation. What sold them was that it worked so quickly and was so easy.

One of my coaching clients, Joy, worked as an LPN in a very busy clinic, handling laboratory patient records. The job was fast-paced and stressful. But it wasn't the pace that made Joy anxious, it was her co-workers. Different personalities and work styles caused tensions. At this point in her life, Joy couldn't quit her job or even transfer. Her health was suffering because of the stress; she couldn't get a good night's sleep, and her blood pressure was on the rise. As her workload did not allow her to take actual breaks, I thought the 3-B-C was a good place to start. Once, doing this at a particularly tense moment at work, Joy experienced a moment of clarity:

> I knew that I would get emotional and angrier if I didn't do something. So instead of trying to fix the toxic individual, I fixed myself. I intentionally relaxed my body and began to take three deep breaths, and immediately felt my body and mind relax. I kept doing this until my mind was in a state of calm in which I could think more clearly and decide between conversations with clear intention, or walk away and take a break. I finally realized what is in my control and what is not. That was a breakthrough for me and my well-being.

I introduced the strategy during the mandatory resilience classes for all employees at our facility. Even the busy health-care workers, who feel they don't have time for a class or even a break, liked it. Often on my resilience walkabouts in the hospital, which are quick reinforcing visits, I hear things like "I'm still breathing!" or "I breathed five times yesterday and stayed calm!"

I've even taught this technique to my teenage children, who have been able to use it when they get stressed or upset, and regain a sense of calm.

trust your gut

THE CUE-2-DO IS MY PERSONAL FAVORITE strategy, and I don't ever want to live without it. It spurs us to change our thinking, which can change our path and improve our health. When I was growing up, my dad used to say, "If you have that gut feeling that something isn't right, then it isn't, and you should do something about it." So I think of the Cue-2-Do as the gut check. I perform a body/mind check and if I notice any discomfort (sometimes in my gut), I ask: What is my cue? What is it signaling? What is the current drama? Is there anything I can do and want to do about it right now?

Changing your thought patterns in times of stress can be very difficult. I coached a nurse on stress-management techniques, to cope with her very busy life (12-hour workdays, being a single parent). She had experienced daily headaches for six months, and wasn't sure of the cause. Of course, I encouraged her to have this checked out. But in the meantime, we explored this with the Cue-2-Do. When thinking about what her cue might be signaling, she told me she was assigned a new supervisor about six months ago. His style was very different from her previous supervisor; he seemed to always be watching her work and correcting her. Using the Cue-2-Do, she then asked herself if she could change the channel. The first thing she did was look inward. She rediscovered that she was a good nurse, and that she shouldn't get frazzled when the supervisor was around. She also told herself that she is thankful to have such a good job. Those thoughts helped her move on to the action part of Cue-2-Do. She decided to confront her supervisor and express her feelings. He had no idea that she was frazzled, and he too thought she was a good nurse. He explained his corrections were to help her sharpen her skills and maintain her competency. Guess what? Her headaches subsided for the most part, but when one did arise she knew that was her cue for action! She saw her physician, and thankfully, it was nothing serious.

just take ten

WHEN I FIRST INTRODUCED THE OASIS 1 STONE STRATEGY to my classes, I thought many would think it too "fluffy." But I was wrong! Many groups have found that this contemplative technique helped them find balance in their stress-filled day. Some providers reported back that they use the 1 Stone to center themselves before a stressful procedure with a patient, and it helps them stay present and relaxed. I've worked with behavioral health workers who have used the technique in the support groups they facilitate for survivors of violence, PTSD, and grief. Holding the stone helps the participants stay calm and balanced.

I have also implemented the 1 Stone in a mini-retreat that my colleagues and I developed for a large group of soldiers and civilians with high-stress jobs working with transitioning military members. The program consists of team-building activities, art for stress relief, massage therapy, music for stress relief and several stress-management techniques to help these individuals maintain their resilience, to bend without breaking in these tough jobs. Here is what some participants said:

> I know that the moment I walk through those doors at work, I won't have a moment to breathe, think or even take a restroom break. I will use this technique while sitting in my car so that I can center myself before the craziness of the day.
>
>
>
> I'm going to use the stone/10-breath technique on the drive home. The traffic is nerve-racking, and when I get home I take my irritation out on my family. This is a meditation I can do because it is quick; I don't have to close my eyes. I will also share this with my family; I think we could all use a way to find a sense of calm and balance.

You don't need a rock; it can be any small object that you can hold and touch. I kept mini-footballs in my office and the workplace relaxation room. Some used them to squeeze their stress away, and others used them as something to help them bring balance back to their hectic day.

letter of love

THE OASIS PRACTICES ARE SIMPLE WAYS to nurture ourselves, something we must never forget! Millie also introduced me to another self-care tool: the act of penning a letter to myself. At the close of a moving, productive session with Millie, she asked our group to write a thank-you note to ourselves, mentioning the positives of our lives and motivating ourselves toward self-care. I felt a little silly writing to myself, but did it anyway. Weeks later I got the letter, addressed to me in my own handwriting. I had forgotten all about sending it. But I will never forget receiving it. You see, it was a very stressful time and I was feeling defeated, with job insecurity, three children on the verge of adulthood, and a husband going through some major life changes. This is what I read:

Dear Angel,

Thank you for who you have become, even through the rough times and rocky paths. I feel that you are a good, loving, supporting mother; you are not perfect, but who is? You do your best to walk with the light of Christ in you. You are not perfect but that's okay. You are a good wife and try your best to be understanding and non-judgmental. You have a blessed life. Continue on!

Wow! That hit me and helped me! My colleagues had received their letters, too. Each one of them had the same epiphany as I did; the letters arrived at the time we needed them the most. Realizing that this was the height of good self-care, I decided to use it in teaching healthcare providers about care and respect for themselves and what they do.

In this super-busy day and age we put off taking care of ourselves, but we shouldn't. Add the OASIS in the Overwhelm 60-second strategies to your self-care plan. It has worked for soldiers, healthcare providers, teenagers, and other folks—you will see results too!

Never worry about numbers.

Help one person at a time, and always start with the person nearest you.

Mother Teresa

REBECCA SANTIAGO, an RN and 30-year health-care veteran, has fostered connections with organizations and individuals. She has given many presentations, participates in research, has written health-related articles, and serves on several boards and councils. She recently co-authored a research study: *Removing Barriers: Creating Health Care Access for Connecticut's Newly Insured.*

Rebecca is currently President of the Hartford Chapter of the National Association of Hispanic Nurses. She received a 2014 Connecticut Hero Award for the *Care We Can Count On* campaign and participated in the *Faces of Hope* campaign for Nurse Navigators.

e-mail: rsantiago1718@gmail.com
website: www.nahnhc.org

oasis—it's not a mirage, it's a miracle!

WHEN I FIRST SAW that we would have an OASIS Training as part of our curriculum for The Graduate Institute Integrative Healing Health Coach and Patient Navigation Graduate Certificate Program, I had no idea what OASIS was. But I was ready to try something new. I have read many books on mindfulness therapy, tried Tai Chi and martial arts, looking for relief and relaxation. But I have always felt something was missing, and nothing really "clicked." After checking out the website, I was hooked. I ordered the *OASIS in the Overwhelm* book, DVD and the 1 Stone package, and was ready and excited to meet Millie.

My entire life has been about caring for others. I am a mom of three boys, helped my mother raise two nephews and two grandnieces, and now have nine grandchildren of my own. I work as a registered nurse reaching out to underserved communities where there are disparities in access to health care, financial issues, behavioral health and chronic disease issues. I am dealing with communities that need so many answers on how to address their complicated lives, that many times I come home so wound up that falling asleep becomes the challenge for the night. Although I love and always have loved what I do, I could never find the time to relax and rejuvenate. I also struggled with what I came to recognize as post-traumatic stress syndrome.

I grew up in the South Bronx in New York. We lived in a two-bedroom apartment in a complex surrounded by abandoned buildings. Those were very turbulent times: there were gang wars, poverty, burning buildings. I still remember hearing gunshots in the night, hiding under the bed, afraid that a stray bullet would hit one of us. As a second-generation Hispanic child, raised to learn how to pray with Catholicism, I was not offered any tools to deal with that deep, ongoing stress. The 1993 and 2001 bombings of the World Trade Center that I and my fellow New Yorkers lived through, and in which I lost close friends, brought up the overwhelming feelings I still harbored from my childhood. It took a long time for me to seek help. I didn't want people to know I had "mental issues"—that stigma was too much for me to handle.

The impetus for finally seeking help was the simultaneous death of my mother and my aunt, to whom I was close. Forty minutes after my mother lost her battle, I received the devastating news that my aunt had passed away from esophageal cancer. These events tipped me over the edge. After the funerals, I fell into a depression and stopped going to work. Finally, my concerned nursing colleagues arranged an "intervention." How I wish that intervention had been with Millie and OASIS, as I believe the healing would then have started from within. Instead, I went to a traditional therapist. I mean no disrespect to her; on a personal level she was a wonderful person. But "talk therapy" meant reliving the pain, with no instrument or strategy to take home to deal with the anxiety and depression. I was referred to a psychiatrist, who immediately prescribed an antidepressant and an anti-anxiety medication—a prescription that I never filled. Speaking with therapists and psychiatrists about the experiences and traumas of my childhood and adult life did not offer me relief. I would relive specific scenes from the past, especially when I experienced stressful situations.

And then OASIS came on my path. After reading what OASIS had done for so many people, I knew in my heart that I had finally found a possible avenue to alleviate the unhealthy stress responses I had been experiencing.

Our weekend trainings were more than I expected. Millie spoke to us as if we were old friends having a reunion, not a cohort group in a graduate certification program. I loved learning and practicing the OASIS Strategies with the others under the guidance of Millie's encouraging voice. She challenged us when we spoke—turning negative statements into statements of positivity.

Incorporating the strategies into my home life, my work, real-life situations, was another thing. When you practice a strategy, you get some idea of what it should do. But when you are in a difficult situation in which your spiritual balance can be tipped in either direction, it is not easy to manage the situation. In two particular instances I used or taught the strategies I saw first-hand that they really work.

One day I was driving to work on my 45-minute commute. I stopped at a red light behind another SUV. All of a sudden, I felt a jolt and then heard an awful crunching sound. The car behind had hit my car with enough force to make it slam into the SUV in front of me. I immediately felt anger rising from the tips of my toes, and wanted to fly out of my car to confront the driver in the vehicle that struck me. But something made me stop. I took a deep breath and exhaled so loudly that the drivers of the cars turned around thinking I was in distress. I took another deep breath and exhaled loudly several times more. I didn't get out of the car until I felt my anger had gone away. I was stunned at how quickly I regained my calm. When I did get out, I approached the drivers with concern, asking if they were all right. We exchanged phone numbers. We decided not to call the police, as the driver who hit my car admitted his fault. My car had front and back damage, but I could still drive, so I continued on to work.

For the rest of my ride, I went over the situation over and over, in amazement. I had been in a similar situation in New York about two years prior. That situation was volatile and didn't end as well as this one. I not only ended up in the emergency room with a severe migraine and whiplash, but it took me a long time to recover, physically and mentally. When the crash happened this time, I felt a déjà vu and thought I would end up in the emergency room again. But now I was armed with a strategy specifically geared to tough situations. The 3-B-C breathing strategy was what made the difference in this potentially escalating situation.

It would be fascinating to have the body scanned with computer tomography during stressful situations and measure the difference between a person who performs this strategy and someone who doesn't. I have no doubt that we would see amazing differences in the body's response to the situation.

The second event involved my seven-year-old grandson, Lucas. Lucas has been staying with us, his grandparents, in Connecticut. He is a sweet young boy who is very emotional and has been labeled as having "anxiety issues." It hasn't been easy at all for him to be away from his parents and adjust to a new school. Yet Lucas has managed very quickly to win the hearts of his teachers with his infectious smile and his love for learning. One night, Lucas wasn't feeling well. He kept telling me, "Yaya, I feel like I have butterflies in my stomach." After assessing his vital signs and by the queasy look on his face, I knew that he was going to vomit at any moment. This is not a pleasant experience for anyone, but Lucas was inconsolable, and his heart was racing. He was obviously very afraid of having to throw up. I went into OASIS mode, and decided to teach him the 3-B-C breathing technique. Children are indeed very open and are sponges for learning. Also, my grandson and I have a strong bond of trust, so I had no doubt that he would pick this up very quickly. And he did. He relaxed and focused as I talked him through the 3-B-C. Remembering Millie's words, "Learn the OASIS Strategies and make them your own," I guided Lucas, asked him to put his hand over his heart, and told him that with each breath, his heart would slow down. My instruction was interrupted often, as he was still throwing up. But every time, I was able to bring him back to focus on what we had started. By the end of this encounter, despite the vomiting episodes, Lucas had learned to breathe and slow down his heart rate.

Another time, Lucas came to me very upset and anxious after a "nightmare." Intuitively, I knew we needed something more than "our" 3-B-C to help him focus. I brought out a bag of stones that I had collected at a local street fair and asked him to pick one. And so began the teaching of the OASIS 1 Stone strategy. Because his heart was racing, again, I used the technique and had him place his hand over his heart, to help him slow down his heart rate. He remembered to take his deep breaths, exhaling deeply as he put all his focus on the shiny green stone he had selected from my bag. By the time we were done, he hugged me and said he wanted to sleep with his stone.

These days, Lucas takes his stone to school and has used the 1 Stone strategy, especially when he gets nervous or upset. His teachers have asked me what I have done. Lucas has had fewer episodes of anxious behavior since he has learned 1 Stone. The teachers have invited me to come teach some of the OASIS Strategies in their special-needs class. Lucas often comes to me and tells me: "Yaya, I can breathe with our stones." Lucas' incredible responsiveness to the strategies has made me realize that children are so malleable and eager and able to learn. These simple interventions offer hope for children who exhibit behavioral or social difficulties.

As I mentioned before, I was raised Catholic. But in recent years I have reconnected with another part of my family that follows the *Yoruban Ifa* tradition, that includes the practice of *Santería.* Many people associate or confuse these religions with witchcraft or *Brujería,* or even satanic or black magic. As I have continued my studies and practice of both religions, I see a great connection with OASIS. I revealed to Millie during one of our sessions that in *Yoruban Ifa* we practice meditation when we want to commune with our ancestors. We use seven clear glasses filled with water and white candles, and are instructed to clear our minds and practice deep breathing to enter into a pure state of clarity and calmness. OASIS is so similar to what we practice that it came very easily to me to calm my anxieties, especially when confronting difficult situations. OASIS has given me another option to use strategies at any time, at any place, without drawing attention to what I am doing.

My journey with OASIS has just started, as has my journey to becoming a health and wellness coach. In preparing my portfolio to submit to the International Coaching Federation, my intention is to emphasize how OASIS has impacted the course of my new and upcoming profession.

There are many situations in which OASIS Strategies can be used—for personal, social and spiritual well-being. As a registered nurse, I have utilized OASIS Strategies with patients who have learned of a cancer diagnosis, one of the most emotional consults anyone can encounter. Millie continues to integrate OASIS into organizations like the police department and so many others, where stress levels are high and stress management can turn potential life-threatening situations around. I would recommend that OASIS be taken into the educational system on all levels, and that organizations, whether profit or nonprofit, offer OASIS courses to their employees.

OASIS: it is not a mirage. It's a miracle. *¡Gracias, Millie!*

note from the editor

IT HAS BEEN A BLAST AND PRIVILEGE to work with these 25 amazing people, all experts in their fields, all passionate and committed "difference makers."

Where I may have helped them find or fine-tune their verbal form, each of them has opened my eyes to a new slice of life and new piece of the OASIS experience. The enthusiasm, power and reach of the O Community are irresistible.

CECILE WIJNE KROON is an Editorial Consultant who helps her clients find clarity and form when they want to publish their ideas.

She is currently working on her book and presentation about The Art of Losing©, for caregivers and care receivers who deal with tough challenges. Cecile explores how all of us can reinvigorate our presence and our connections when we acknowledge our full experience.

Cecile is also an educator, linguist, mother of two, and producer with award-winning filmmaker and husband Piet Kroon. She has lived with multiple sclerosis for 15+ years. Born and raised in The Netherlands, Cecile moved to Los Angeles in 1995 and presently lives and works in Connecticut.

e-mail: cecilewk@me.com

WENDY PERROTTI
wendy@wendyperrotti.com
www.wendyperrotti.com

STEVE PORCARO
Steve@14Allcoaching.com
www.salesplusmvp.com

JEAN STETZ-PUCHALSKI
info@individualdifferences.com
www.individualdifferences.com

MORGAN BLANTON
artisansalonfalmouth@gmail.com
www.artisansalonfalmouth.com

KAREN SENTEIO
uncover.your.verve@snet.net
www.vimandverve.net

JERRY SINNAMON
jasinnamon@aol.com
www.be-on-purpose.com

millie's acknowledgments

ABUNDANT THANKS to the myriads of people who have given me—and continue to give me—oases throughout my life:

- 🌴 the folks pictured on the left who are members of the OASIS "Kitchen Cabinet" and who assist in training many new OASIS Facilitators;

- 🌴 friends and colleagues in Latin America, Europe, the Philippines, Myanmar, the USA;

- 🌴 teachers whose wisdom continues to feed us all, especially Thich Nhat Hanh, Jon Kabat-Zinn, Ilana Rubenfeld, Francine Shapiro, and Lous Verdier;

- 🌴 the many clients whose wrestling with "Big T Traumas" and "little t traumas" continue to push us to dive deeper and wider;

- 🌴 the worldwide OASIS Community whose support and compassion strengthen and inspire on a daily basis;

- 🌴 our O Community liaison Renee O'Connell and our ever-steady advisors Tom Campbell and Terry Nolan;

- 🌴 the 25 people who contributed chapters to this book;

- 🌴 our colossal editor Cecile Wijne Kroon, who orchestrated the wildly-varying voices of these 25 into a melodious symphony;

- 🌴 and to the Source of all being, for our precious lives and for the opportunity to use our days on earth in ways that are unique to each of us.

4·D

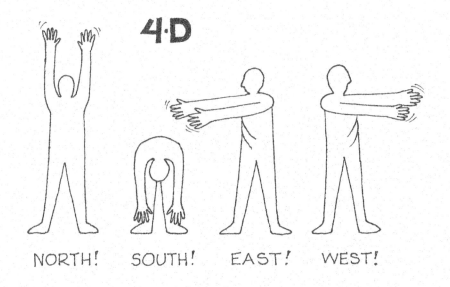

NORTH!   SOUTH!   EAST!   WEST!

4-D = Four-Directions

stretch your body

1. Stand up.

2. Feel your connection to the earth.

3. Stretch your arms and whole body *north* to the heavens. Say out loud the *north-south-east-west* words as you do each direction.

4. Bend down—*south*—to the earth.

5. Stand again.

6. Stretch to the *east*—as far as you can.

7. Stretch to the *west*. Scan the total horizon.

3BC

STOP THE HAMSTER WHEEL!

1   2   3

E M E R G E N C Y

REPEAT
2 MORE
TIMES

P R E V E N T I V E

TAKE IN
COLOR OR OBJECT

- HANDS
ON BELLY

INHALE 3X
THE FEELING
OF COLOR
OR OBJECT

NOTICE
HOW
YOU
FEEL

3-B-C = Three-Breath-Coutdown

calm your mind

1. Stop the whirl. Wherever you are, give yourself some psychic space. Put both hands on your belly.

2. *Preventive*: begin with an inhale. Take in something pleasurable.

3. *Emergency*: begin with an exhale. Let go of anger, worry, agitation. Make room for calmness.

4. Take three deep breaths, slowly, gently.

5. Give yourself time to enjoy the slow-down.

CUE·2·DO

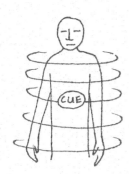

SCAN FOR
PHYSICAL CUES
⬆1⬆

IDENTIFY THE
EMOTIONAL CHANNEL
& DRAMA
⬆2⬆

TAKE ACTION
OR
CHANGE CHANNELS
⬆3⬆

Cue-2-Do

change your brain

When you're upset or angry, notice exactly where you feel it in your body or mind. Then ask yourself the five questions:

1. What is my cue right now?

2. What is that cue signaling: what channel am I on?

3. What's the current drama on that channel?

4. Is there anything I can do and want to do right now about the situation?

5. What action is best for me right now? Make a conscious choice. Take definite action.

1 STONE

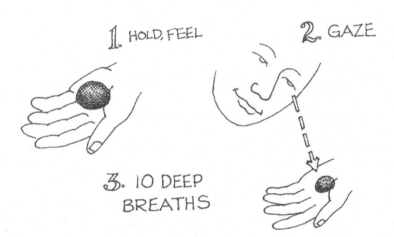

1. HOLD, FEEL

2. GAZE

3. 10 DEEP BREATHS

1 Stone

balance your total self

1. Take a stone—or any object. Hold it in your hand.

2. With your eyes open, breathe in and out, slowly, ten times.

3. Allow space for your mind to do the rinse cycle.

4. Let in the larger picture.

5. Enjoy your oasis.

more oasis for you

OASIS in the Overwhelm: 60-second strategies for balance in a busy world **Book** $19.95

Looking for calm in the chaos? Learn four powerful 60-second strategies that can instantly reduce stress, strengthen your physical, emotional, intellectual and spiritual well-being. Read how the latest in neuroscience research verifies their effectiveness. Use these strategies to become healthier and happier, easily, quickly. 171 pp.

OASIS in the Overwhelm **Audio CD** $19.95

Too busy to read? Your chance to listen and learn, even as you drive. Quickly become less stressed, more effective—and happier—at work and at home. Step-by-step instruction on how to do the strategies, narrated by Millie Grenough. Includes information about neuroplasticity and tips for use in different situations, at home, at work, and on the road. 14 cuts, 75 minutes.

OASIS in the Overwhelm 28 Day Guide: Rewire Your Brain from Chaos to Calm **Book** $20.95

Rewire your brain from chaos to calm in just 28 days. This manual provides you with creative suggestions for day-to-day actions to help you master the 60-second strategies and incorporate them into your daily life. Includes preparatory warm-up material, self-assessment prior to beginning, ample space for noting progress. 112 pp.

Got Chaos? Get Calm! DVD $15.95

Got Chaos? Need a Quick Fix to Calmness? This DVD provides exactly that: 14 To-the-Point-Videos to help you stay sane in a crazy world. 60 seconds is all it takes. Why wait? Each brief video demonstrates how to perform the strategy plus the science supporting it and the benefits from doing it. Perfect for plugging in to when you have only a few minutes. Choose your strategy to fit your need! 14 videos, each 2 to 5 minutes.

O to Go pack $9

Take OASIS with you! This convenient O to Go pack includes everything you need to do the strategies on the road, including directions and your own stone. All tucked into an OASIS zippered key chain coin purse. A perfect gift for a stressed-out child or adult, a colleague on overdrive, an anxious family member—and wonderful to give to yourself, too. 3" x 4¼".

🌴 *OASIS* book/CD/DVD by Millie Grenough.

🌴 *OASIS 28 Day Guide* by Millie Grenough, Jill Berquist, & Virginia Kravitz.

🌴 *OASIS* book and *28 Day Guide* also available as eBooks.

Discounts for combined purchases of five or more items.

Quantity discounts available for bulk purchases for educational use, premiums, fundraising, sales promotions.

Contact: orders@beaverhillpress.com

oasis en español

OASIS en la adversidad: estrategias de 60 segundos para alcanzar el equilibrio en un mundo agitado. Libro $16.95

¿Buscas tranquilidad en medio del caos? Date 60 segundos para alcanzar el equilibrio. En este libro enconcontrarás información applicable y sencilla que te ayudarás a tranquilizar tu mente en tu recorrido a lo largo de toda la vida. ¿Es possible encontrar la paz en una vida agitada? ¡Sí se puede! 157 pp.

🌴 Autora: Millie Grenough.

🌴 Traducción: Dra. Caroline Jane Cooke.

OASIS en la Adversidad Guía de 28 Días: Redirige Tu Cerebro del Caos a la Tranquilidad Libro $20.95

¿Excesivamente ocupado? ¿No tienes tiempo para nada más? Regálate un *OASIS*. En el breve lapso de 28 días, reemplaza los antiguos hábitos que te mantienen "paralizado" con nuevos patrones de conducta poderosos y agradables. La *Guía* te enseñará como apartar algunos minutos de tu día de tal manera que las Estrategias OASIS sean parte de tu vida de una manera fácil y segura. Siente la diferencia en tu salud y en el factor felicidad.

🌴 Autoras: Millie Grenough con Jill Berquist
   y Virginia Kravitz.

🌴 Traducción: Dra. Caroline Jane Cooke.

🌴 Ahora disponible en versión eBook.

how to reach us

For trainings, workshops, presentations, retreats, coaching
conducted by Millie Grenough:
www.milliegrenough.com
millie@milliegrenough.com

For coaching and presentations
by other Authorized OASIS Facilitators:
see their bio pages in this book for contact information.

To share your story:
stories@beaverhillpress.com

To order books and other OASIS products:
orders@beaverhillpress.com
www.beaverhillpress.com

Discounts for combined purchases of five or more items.

Quantity discounts available for bulk purchases for
educational use, premiums, fundraising, sales promotions.

Contact: orders@beaverhillpress.com

index

CPSIA information can be obtained at www.ICGtesting.com
Printed in the USA
BVOW09s1553120115

382743BV00007B/34/P